D1300688

100 GREATEST TRIPS

Bai Sao beach, on the southeast coast of Vietnam's Phu Quoc island.

TRAVEL +LEISURE

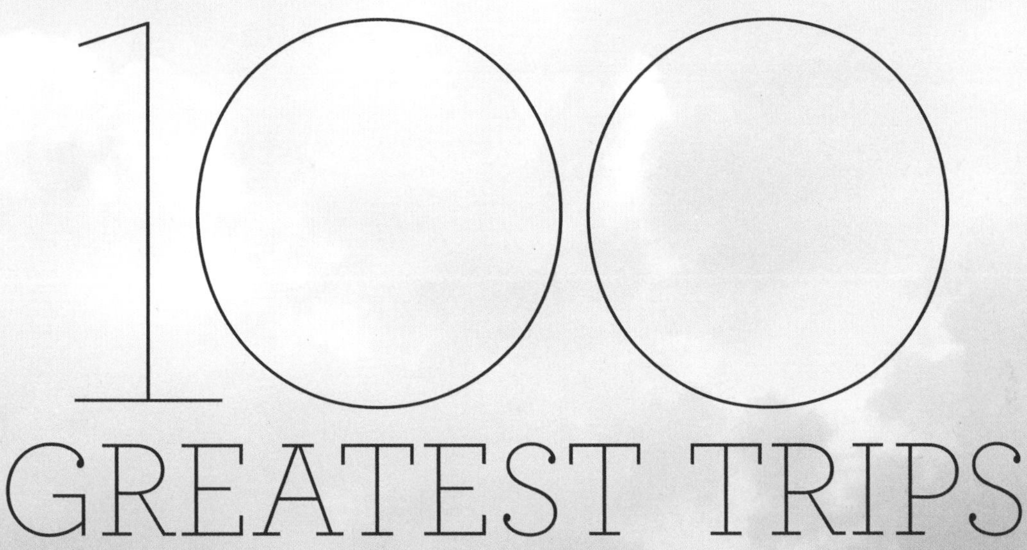

100 GREATEST TRIPS

FROM THE EDITORS OF THE WORLD'S LEADING TRAVEL MAGAZINE

THIRD EDITION

TRAVEL +LEISURE BOOKS

AMERICAN EXPRESS PUBLISHING CORPORATION
NEW YORK

TRAVEL + LEISURE
100 GREATEST TRIPS
THIRD EDITION

Editor Margot Guralnick
Art Director Leigh Nelson
Project Editors Peter Jon Lindberg, Jane Margolies, Maria Shollenbarger
Assistant Managing Editor Meeghan Truelove
Production Manager David Richey
Photo Editor Robyn Lange
Assistant Book Editor Alison Goran
Design Associate Colin Tunstall
Reporters Ken Baron, Jessica Dineen, Amy Goldwasser, Mario López-Cordero, Carolina A. Miranda, Kathryn O'Shea-Evans, Michael Sandler, Tom Zoellner
Copy Editors Diego Hadis, Jane Halsey, Edward Karam
Researchers Robert Alford, Adam Bisno, Anila Churi, Holiday Dmitri, Erin Florio, Julia Houlihan, Yelena Moroz, Bryan Pirolli, Letizia Rossi, Paola Singer, Mary Staub

TRAVEL + LEISURE
Editor-in-Chief Nancy Novogrod
Creative Director Nora Sheehan
Executive Editor Jennifer Barr
Deputy Editor Laura Begley
Managing Editor Mike Fazioli
Arts/Research Editor Mario R. Mercado
Copy Chief Lee Magill
Photo Editor Katie Dunn
Production Director Rosalie Abatemarco-Samat
Production Manager Ayad Sinawi

AMERICAN EXPRESS PUBLISHING CORPORATION
President, C.E.O. Ed Kelly
S.V.P., Chief Marketing Officer Mark V. Stanich
C.F.O., S.V.P., Corporate Development & Operations Paul B. Francis
V.P., General Manager Keith Strohmeier, Frank Bland

V.P., Books & Products, Publisher Marshall Corey
Director, Book Programs Bruce Spanier
Director, Customer Retention & Loyalty Greg D'Anca
Senior Marketing Manager, Branded Books Eric Lucie
Assistant Marketing Manager Lizabeth Clark
Director of Fulfillment & Premium Value Phil Black
Manager of Customer Experience & Product Development Charles Graver
Director of Finance Tom Noonan
Associate Business Manager Desiree Bernardez
Corporate Production Manager Stuart Handelman

Cover design by Leigh Nelson
Cover photograph by Blasius Erlinger

ISBN 978-0-7566-4103-0 | ISSN 1933-1231

Published by American Express Publishing Corporation
1120 Avenue of the Americas, New York, New York 10036
With Contributions and Distributed by DK Publishing, Inc.,
375 Hudson Street, New York, New York 10014
Manufactured in China

Bellhop Ly Rany at the Raffles Hotel Le Royal, in Phnom Penh.

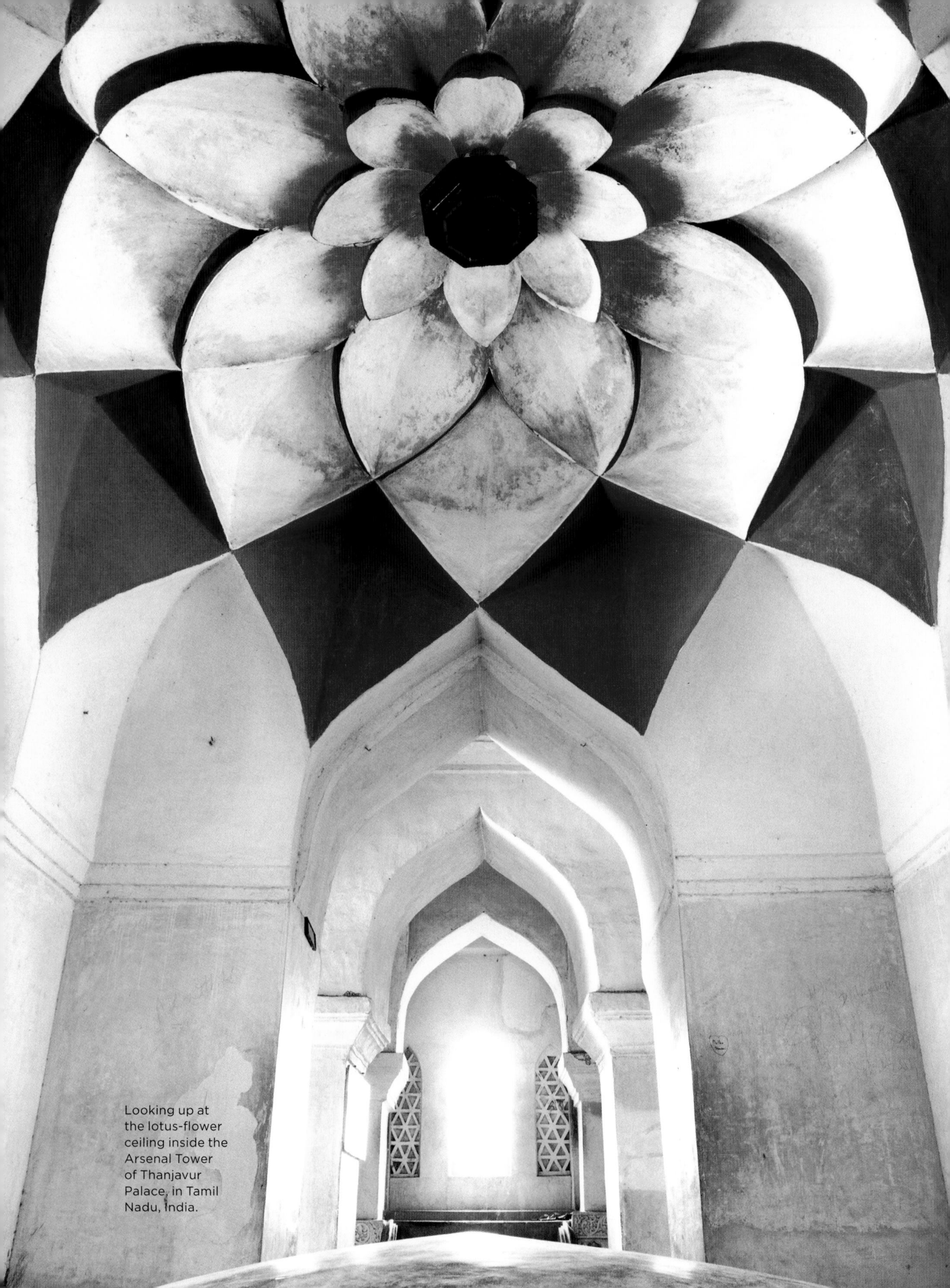

Looking up at the lotus-flower ceiling inside the Arsenal Tower of Thanjavur Palace, in Tamil Nadu, India.

CONTENTS

The pool and grounds at Château les Merles in Mouleydier, just outside Bordeaux, France.

On Calle Cochera del Hobo, in the Old Town section of Cartagena, Colombia.

INTRODUCTION

As someone who is always on a trip, just back from a trip, or planning a trip, I am not quite ready to anoint any one as the greatest of them all. Why limit myself to a single favorite destination or travel experience when I have such a deserving group of contenders to choose from—summer vacations by the sea in Italy, hiking trips in Chile and Bhutan, an upcoming sojourn to Patagonia my family will be taking next winter. So the expansiveness of a book such as this, with dozens of different travel adventures, in Vermont, Vietnam, Moscow, New Zealand, and places beyond and in between, seems to me not only handy but entirely appropriate.

If you're a reader of *Travel + Leisure* magazine, you may well recognize many of the places and images featured within this book. It's the third of our *100 Greatest Trips* compendiums, which my editors and I put together each year. Our intent is simple: to assemble a broad and inspiring range of travel ideas, lay them out geographically by region, and tie it all up at the back of the book with our Guide section, featuring maps and related resource listings for pertinent hotels, restaurants, shops, museums, and more. The result of an intensive culling process that stretches from twelve months' worth of T+L issues to our seven international editions, the stories chosen for this volume represent both the timely (making the restaurant rounds in Las Vegas) and the timeless (touring the art-encrusted temples and historic sites of India's Tamil Nadu). There are lesser-known destinations such as the former Eastern Bloc city of Kiev in Ukraine, now undergoing a transformation with the infusion of international investments; get-away-from-it-all opportunities in Spain's Andalusia, the Aveyron in France, and Dominica and Saba in the Caribbean; and high-energy urban spots ranging from Tokyo to Brooklyn, New York.

Lucky for us, the world keeps offering up new wonders to explore: off-the-beaten-path neighborhoods with authentic and distinct appeal, once remote areas made accessible through improved transportation, and regions now reopened after years of political turmoil. In the end, the goal of this book, like that of the magazine, is to stimulate travel. For, as we like to say at T+L, travel changes you—and you change the world.

By Nancy Novogrod, Editor-in-Chief

A country lane flanked by two paddocks at a horse farm in Middleburg, Virginia.

UNITED STATES + CANADA

Provincetown

PLAYING LIGHTHOUSE KEEPER ON CAPE COD

On an empty stretch of sand on the northernmost tip of Cape Cod sits an unusual way to beat Provincetown's summer crowds: the Race Point Lighthouse, a working beacon with a keeper's house and outlying cottage open to overnight guests. The property looks much as it did a century ago, thanks to the American Lighthouse Foundation, whose on-site volunteers attend to the buildings and, from May to mid-October, the guests who are staying over. Choose among three decidedly Yankee bedrooms under the eaves in the 1879 keeper's residence, all with lace curtains, braided rugs, and patchwork quilts. (The lighthouse's first keeper slept in the Green Room.) For weeklong stays, move into the newly renovated two-bedroom Whistle House, which sleeps eight and once held the steam-powered foghorn and bell.

There was a time when every ship captain sailing south from Boston looked to the beacon for a safe pass by the point, known and named for its powerful race, or crosscurrent. The lighthouse, in continuous operation since 1816, is automated now, and visitors can twirl up its spiral stairs for a 360-degree >>

Race Point Lighthouse and its keeper's house. Opposite, from far left: Lopes Square in downtown Provincetown; a lobster roll from one of the town's fish shacks.

T+L Tip
From April through November, local outfit Art's Dune Tours leads excursions to Cape Cod National Seashore. Along the way you'll pass the former beach cottages of such writers as Tennessee Williams and Eugene O'Neill.

Trolling in Provincetown's harbor, above. Above right: On Race Point Beach.

view of the cape. The beachfront compound sits four miles out of town and off the road: you cross the dunes in a four-wheel-drive or have the ALF staff pick you up in theirs.

En route, take in the scene in Provincetown. Clem & Ursie's is the spot for steamed lobster, and Ciro & Sal's serves Northern Italian dishes, such as Abruzzese, a sauté of local cod, scallops, clams, and mussels over linguine. The area around MacMillan Wharf is home to lobster roll shacks and the Whydah Museum, which displays treasures from North America's only excavated pirate shipwreck. You can kayak or take a sailing lesson at Flyer's Boat Rentals, or grab wheels from Ptown Bikes and cruise the 5.2-mile loop between Herring Cove and Race Point Beach. Don't forget groceries on your way out of town—at the lighthouse, you can cook meals in the shared kitchen. Plus, spend days whale-watching, fishing, swimming, combing for seashells, and snuggling into the warm dunes, here at the end of the world. ✚

GUIDE, PAGE 257.

Monadnock Region

NEW ENGLAND COUNTRY LIFE

THE NATIONAL TRUST calls Keene "a Currier & Ives landscape come to life," which, if you disregard the skateboard park, is pretty spot-on. Broad, elm-shaded Main Street has cafés, lively bars, and the landmark Colonial Theatre. In autumn, the surrounding countryside is just as big a draw. Take it in from the top of 3,165-foot Mount Monadnock, which has views clear to Boston, Maine, and Vermont. (Allow three hours for the hike to the summit and back.) Then drive Route 12 to check out the lovely Greek Revival architecture of nearby Walpole, the pristine town where Ken Burns has his film studio. Don't miss chocolate artisan Larry Burdick's headquarters, L.A. Burdick, a combination confectionery and bistro where you can take chocolate-cooking classes.

Return to Keene via Route 10 to pass through four covered bridges. Spend the night at the E.F. Lane Hotel, carved out of an old downtown department store, or the Inn at Valley Farms, a 1774 colonial manse with an organic farm adjoining an orchard. Time your visit for October's Keene Pumpkin Festival when, in an annual attempt to set a world record, towers displaying an astonishing number of carved jack-o'-lanterns rise above the town square. ✚

GUIDE, PAGE 257.

The 1859 Cresson Bridge, just south of Keene.

Vermont

THE GREEN MOUNTAIN STATE'S WINTER WONDERLAND

Twin Farms' Log Cabin, in Barnard, above. Above left: Snowshoeing in Barnard. Opposite: The view from Lincoln Peak, at Sugarbush, in Warren.

NO SEASON better defines this "narrow, pinched-up state on the wrong side of Boston"—as Bette Davis called it—than winter, when ice goblins cover granite ridges and only the license plates are evergreen. Despite efforts in recent decades to make it more accessible (two four-lane highways, the expansion of Burlington International Airport), Vermont remains caught in a unique—and providential—time warp: a boho Shangri-la populated by graying hippie poets, pastoral activists, and youthful disciples of snowboarding pioneer Jake Burton.

The entire state is remarkably free of visual clutter. In 1970, the Vermont legislature passed the Land Use and Development Law, which still restricts just about every vulgar and unsightly thing man can impose on a natural or historic landscape, including billboards, cell towers, neon lights, subdivisions, and congested highways. The northern half of the state—from Barnard to Stowe, 40 miles south of the Canadian border—is nearly untouched. You can spot moose tracks, drive roads lined with tapped sugar maples, and walk past inky-dark streams in the wilderness with a guide sporting sinew-and-ash bentwood snowshoes.

That's not to say that Vermont doesn't have its frills. In the town of Warren, the Pitcher Inn, done up in dignified country-house style and featuring a Victorian billiards table, is right across from the Warren Store, where you can pick up local Gorgonzola and >>

Off Route 12, outside Barnard, above. Opposite, clockwise from top left: Extreme skier John Egan at Sugarbush; a moose head at the Topnotch Resort & Spa; inside the Barnard General Store; local cheeses at the Warren Store.

a bottle of Opus One. Twin Farms, one of the country's most lavish rural resorts, in Barnard, has a two-to-one staff-to-guest ratio, plus cabins and cottages with interiors that evoke New England (hot cocoa with housemade marshmallows, downy comforters on hickory-twig beds, views of Mount Ascutney) or Morocco (mosaic-tile fireplace, moucharaby window screens). And Topnotch Resort, in Stowe, has a 35,000-square-foot spa.

Famed ski resorts Sugarbush and Stowe have both received green-minded upgrades. For Sugarbush's new post-and-beam base lodge, restaurant, and slopeside condominiums (disguised as a supersize barn), timber was cleared using a team of horses rather than bulldozers. Stowe added a gondola that connects its two mountains, and has just put the finishing touches on a well-appointed, 139-room hotel, the Stowe Mountain Lodge at Spruce Peak, which will complete its new alpine village. The resort then promptly allocated more than 2,000 acres to a permanent conservation easement, preserving part of what makes ski season here surpassingly alluring: woods so still, you can hear the snow falling. ✚

GUIDE, PAGE 257.

Brooklyn

A NEW CHAPTER FOR A STORIED BOROUGH

The Brooklyn Bridge, viewed from Dumbo. Opposite, from left: Carroll Gardens' Bird; Manager Franck Alexandre at Bar Tabac, in Boerum Hill.

ONE IN SEVEN Americans can supposedly trace their roots back to Brooklyn. Yet there are denizens of Manhattan who still link the place with Ralph Kramden, egg creams, and the Dodgers. Get with it! Brooklyn is now a byword for cool—and for boutique shopping and chef-run restaurants with a DIY aesthetic.

New York City's most populous borough covers 73 square miles. On its northern border, overlooking the East River, is the design-art-rock-'n'-roll district of Williamsburg. To the south, near the Brooklyn and Manhattan bridges, are the lively adjoining neighborhoods of Carroll Gardens, Boerum Hill, Cobble Hill, Brooklyn Heights, and Dumbo. At the southern shore sits formerly industrial Red Hook. Inland lie family-focused Park Slope and Prospect Heights.

Williamsburg gets the most hits worldwide, so start there. Though it's known for all things fast-forward, first take a step back: Peter Luger, >>

Alfresco dining at Frankies 457 Spuntino, in Carroll Gardens, below. Below right: A Hasidic resident of Williamsburg.

probably New York's best steak house, has been a culinary standard bearer since the 19th century. Fortified, you're ready to browse the 21st. Need salt-and-pepper shakers shaped like deer heads? Try the Future Perfect.

Decoration problems solved, on to wardrobe: the impeccably curated Bird has outposts in Cobble Hill and Park Slope. Sleep, in Williamsburg, has a sumptuous bed in its storefront window and stocks flirty high-end lingerie.

Next meal? At Franny's, in Prospect Heights, the brick-oven pizza is transcendent. In Carroll Gardens, Frankies 457 Spuntino serves Italian fare as subtle as it is satisfying. Go to Red Hook for delicious Korean-French fusion at the Good Fork.

For cocktails, head to Bar Tabac on Smith Street, a European-style restaurant row spanning Boerum Hill and Carroll Gardens. Bring on the night with explosive funk at Williamsburg's Zebulon, a sultry lounge tucked alongside a motorcycle repair shop, or Barbès, in Park Slope, an unerringly cool club where live bands run the gamut from washboard swing to klezmer. On weekends, suss out Jalopy Theatre, a jazz-bluegrass joint at the edge of the Columbia Waterfront district, just two blocks from the shipping docks (check out the Manhattan skyline, too). Make it here, and it's settled: you've cracked the Brooklyn code. ✚

GUIDE, PAGE 257.

Philadelphia

UP-TO-THE-MINUTE SHOPPING IN OLD CITY

THE SMALL ENCLAVE of old city sits where William Penn founded his original Quaker settlement. It was here, they say, that Ben Franklin tied a key to a kite and Betsy Ross crafted the first American flag. And it is here, just blocks from Independence Hall, that avant-garde clothiers and dealers in Modernist housewares have now set up shop, drawing design and fashion devotees to cobbled streets lined with Colonial residences and 19th-century warehouses.

The paradigms for this chic new breed are Vagabond and Third Street Habit—the former known for cutting-edge labels like Twinkle by Wenlan, the latter for Sonia Rykiel. The sneaker set heads to the men's shop Deep Sleep for Flying Coffin tees. Reform Vintage Modern stocks Raymond Loewy china. Bruges Home is all about the mix, from African game boards to sleek contemporary side chairs.

Come nightfall, the style brigade has plenty of choices. At Continental, a 1960's diner retooled as a martini bar, Sichuan shoestring fries star on a menu of international tapas. Fork gracefully combines seasonal local ingredients with global flavors. Where to bed down? The Sheraton Society Hill is set on a tree-lined drive near the Greek Revival–style Philadelphia Merchant's Exchange; the hotel's low profile matches the cozy scale of this most intimate of neighborhoods. ✚

GUIDE, PAGE 258.

Owner January Bartle at her store, Third Street Habit, in Old City, above left. Above right: Bell-jar sculptures at Bruges Home.

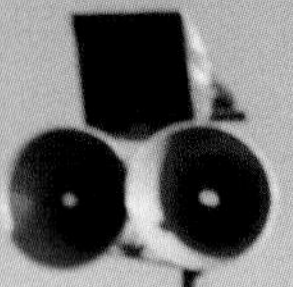

Northern Virginia

DAYS OF WINE AND RACES

At the annual International Gold Cup steeplechase, just south of Middleburg, above. Opposite: Spectators and tailgaters at the racing event.

IN WASHINGTON, D.C., the jockeying is all political, but drive some 50 miles south and you'll find the real thing, in the heart of Virginia's horse country. Ever since Thomas Jefferson built Monticello here, the pastoral foothills of the Blue Ridge Mountains have been a sporting ground for a certain class of power players—folks like the Mellons, Harrimans, Grahams, Jackie Kennedy—coming down to weekend with their thoroughbreds and beagles.

The region's social calendar still revolves around the International Gold Cup and Virginia Gold Cup steeplechases, run every October and May, respectively, on vast, impossibly green rolling plains. A newer attraction is the burgeoning winery scene. Right in the racing town of Middleburg is Chrysalis Vineyards, where visitors are encouraged to cook out on the property's iron grills. Founded in 1997 with the mandate to make the native Virginian grape Norton viable for wine production, the estate puts out a fine Petit Manseng, a Sauternes-like elixir that superbly pairs with foie gras for Gold Cup tailgating. Head south past countless horse farms to Charlottesville, and you encounter some of the state's best chefs and best bottles. The Clifton Inn's Dean Maupin serves innovative comfort food such as pear-and-pecorino ravioli, and at the Kluge Estate, the 2002 brut sparkler, a 100-percent Chardonnay cuvée with crisp green-apple flavors, is a golden cup worth chasing. ✚

GUIDE, PAGE 258.

Cumberland Island

BACK TO NATURE, THE CARNEGIE WAY

JOHN F. KENNEDY JR. and Carolyn Bessette put secluded Cumberland Island on the map when they chose it as the site of their wedding in 1996. The lure: more than 17 miles of pristine woodland, marsh, and beaches just a quick ferry ride from mainland Georgia and Florida. Andrew Carnegie's brother Thomas purchased most of the island in 1881 and bequeathed it to his wife; their children eventually gave it to the National Park Service. And the wildlife is nothing less than extraordinary. Tearing along on a bicycle across miles of hard-packed beach, or following trails fringed

with clattering low fans of saw palmetto, you'll spot wild horses roaming free, armadillos, sea turtles, and some of the island's 335 species of birds, 15 to 20 of which are rare or endangered.

Greyfield Inn, a four-story waterfront estate, is Cumberland Island's sole hotel; its owners—descendants of the Carnegies—have preserved its Cheeveresque charm while subtly introducing up-to-date amenities. The portraits on the walls are of family members and the deep mohair and velvet sofas are reconditioned originals, but the air-conditioning is on, and there's a staff member for every guest.

Lunch at the inn comes in a picnic basket—take it to go or eat on the lawn—while dinner is a formal affair, with dishes such as pork chops with black-eyed peas, swiss chard, and an apple-cider gastrique served in the old dining room. When dusk falls and the last day visitor heads home, guests at Greyfield savor the rare privilege of having an island all to themselves. ✚

GUIDE, PAGE 258.

Greyfield Inn, above. From far left: A wild horse grazes at Christmas Creek; the route from the inn to the beach.

Vero Beach

HOW FLORIDIANS SPELL "EASY COASTAL GETAWAY"

McKee Botanical Garden, above. Above left: Morning at the Driftwood Inn. Opposite: Vero Beach Resort's main attraction.

On Florida's Atlantic shore, not far from the sensory overload of Orlando and the countdowns of Cape Canaveral, lies a quiet, nearly secret coastal outpost. There are no hour-long lines in Vero Beach, no hyper hordes of children. Instead, you'll find the simple pleasures of an old-fashioned seaside town, including the beach—dubbed Velcro Beach, because no one ever wants to leave its crowd-free white sand.

Vero lies partially on a barrier island, with the ocean for its front yard and a river for its back. The Indian River flows past the McKee Botanical Garden, an 18-acre jungle hammock that harbors egrets and herons and lots of lizards. Ocean Drive, the minuscule main drag, where you can find swimsuits in tropical colors, caters to the local golf-and-tennis set (retired racket star Ivan Lendl and his golf-champ daughters have a place in town).

To fully experience quirky Vero, take a room at the Driftwood Inn. Built in 1934 by do-it-yourself developer Waldo Sexton, this oceanfront property is a fantastical marvel of driftwood and rough planks embellished with stained glass, Victorian tiles, and giant bells. For family fun, check into the Vero Beach Resort, Disney's only Florida hotel not at Disney World. Waterslides and mini golf await. And if you want to dip into Walt's world, less than two hours away, you can do it in a day: arrive for the 9 a.m. opening, hit a few major rides, take the Monorail, buy mouse ears. Then hightail it back to Velcro Beach. ✚

GUIDE, PAGE 258.

In front of a Seaside beach pavilion, below. Right: One of the town's retro cottages. Opposite: The community's Interfaith Chapel.

Seaside

THE UTOPIA NOSTALGIA BUILT

SEASIDE IS MANY THINGS. It's a waterfront community on Florida's Panhandle. It's a cluster of pastel-hued bungalows and miniature antebellum-style mansions. It's the foundation of New Urbanism, a contemporary design movement that seeks to tame suburban sprawl with 100-year-old ideas about town planning. And it's a successful revival of the simple life of the best midcentury beach towns. Seaside was founded in 1981 yet it feels timeless: first-class fakery that's genuinely beautiful. It has a superb white-sand beach and a well-thought-out street plan: 80 acres of front gardens spilling native foliage onto welcoming sidewalks. It's an original that became a best-selling formula, triggering some 600 copycat communities nationwide—including several that are within biking distance.

To get in on the fantasy, book a cottage or an apartment in balconied Dreamland Heights, or stay at Seaside's Vera Bradley–designed Inn by the Sea. Vacations here are for family swims, concerts on the green, and burgers at sunset on the roof deck of Bud & Alley's. What else? Rent a classic Schwinn and ride the bike path eight miles along coastal Route 30A to Seaside spin-off Rosemary Beach, an enclave of West Indian–style bungalows. Stop by Onano for a lunch of fresh grouper or cioppino. Take note of the community's new Hotel Saba—your lodging for next year's blast to the past? ✚

GUIDE, PAGE 258.

The 94-year-old Napoleon House Bar & Café, in the French Quarter.

New Orleans

A CITY ON THE REBOUND

IT'S THERE IN THE FLICKER of a gas lamp, in the entangled scents of jasmine and sweet olive, in the caterwaul of a trombone. So much of what you came for in the days before Hurricane Katrina, you come for now: the Garden District mansions; the St. Charles streetcar; the air so soft you're inclined to reach for a spoon. Confine yourself to the tourist playground—from the French Quarter to the zoo—and you might never be reminded that the worst natural disaster in American history happened here.

And yet four years on, the storm has become part of the visitor's agenda. Tour buses make stops in the obliterated Lower Ninth Ward, where the wreckage still sits, shocking to behold. The good news is that there's an enormous amount of energy and many new faces in New Orleans—architects, urban planners, entrepreneurs, academics. Musicians displaced by the storm are returning; Kermit Ruffins and his BBQ Swingers still blow the roof off Vaughan's bar every Thursday. And there are signs of progress. Mardi Gras attendance is close to pre-hurricane levels. Casinos are booming. And the culinary scene has decidedly recovered. New restaurants well worth a visit include Cochon, for chef Donald Link's down-home Cajun Southern cooking; Lüke, a chic brasserie straight out of fin-de-siècle Vienna; and Café Minh, offering Vietnamese-French fusion.

Should you make the pilgrimage? By all means. Come to rebuild houses with the St. Bernard Project, a charitable organization that raises funds to buy construction materials and recruits volunteers to use them. Come to drink Pimm's cups at Napoleon House, a sepia-toned landmark that has more atmosphere than twenty of your hometown bars. Come to pick sides in the who-has-the-best-po'-boys debate (do you prefer Franky & Johnny's or Domilise's?). Come to show your children what jazz is. Come to bear witness to heartbreaking devastation—and to the inspired healing of a city on the rise. ✚

GUIDE, PAGE 258.

T+L Tip

Some New Orleans hotels offer voluntourism packages. At the five Marriott properties, a "care concierge" can recommend community service options. The Ritz-Carlton provides transportation to relief organization sites. Check out opportunities at neworleanscvb.com.

Dallas

BUILDING THE FUTURE IN THE HEART OF TEXAS

DALLAS IS SO RICH in symbols and stereotypes—oil tycoons; the grassy knoll; Southfork; the Cowboys, both NFL and lowercase—that it has become as much a psychological destination as a physical one. Everyone seems to have an image of this town, long before they visit it themselves. It's a brash, muscular, immodest metropolis that believes in putting on a show.

And nowhere is the show more evident than in the city's architecture. Design has long driven Dallas's identity, going back to I. M. Pei's City

Mark Di Suvero's *Ave* (1973), outside the thriving Dallas Museum of Art.

Hall, begun in 1965, and Philip Johnson's 1970 John F. Kennedy Memorial Plaza, a luminous declaration of architecture's power. Now it's making news here again. Santiago Calatrava—the ultimate architectural hired gun—is creating three epic bridges for the Trinity River Corridor Project, which may finally give Dallas the kind of grand, central public space that draws people to San Antonio and Austin. One span will be 40 stories tall, the local equivalent of the St. Louis Gateway Arch.

The same outsize scope can be found downtown, which is being reimagined by a staggering array of marquee names. The Arts District, with the Dallas Museum of Art (DMA) for its cornerstone, will, by 2009, have buildings by four Pritzker Prize-winning architects fronting one street: I. M. Pei's Meyerson Symphony Center; Renzo Piano's Nasher Sculpture Center; and Rem Koolhaas's and Norman Foster's additions to the Dallas Center for the Performing Arts. Meanwhile, the city's arts scene has been reenergized by a $400 million-plus gift (from a consortium of local collectors) to the DMA. The breadth of the donation—1,200 pieces, including work by such postwar masters as Jackson Pollock and Jasper Johns, and sizable holdings in Arte Povera—is remarkable, and in keeping with the city's de facto slogan: Live large, think big. ✚

GUIDE, PAGE 259.

Hamilton County

PLAY FRONTIER PIONEER FOR THE WEEKEND

MOST VISITORS to Conner Prairie—an open-air living history museum just north of Indianapolis—spend a few hours roaming about, touring the Indian trading post, the smithy, and other 19th-century buildings linked by the 850-acre property's gravel paths. But participants in the overnight program "Weekend on the Farm" really turn back the clock. Each guest dons a costume (aprons and bonnets for women and girls, overalls and kerchiefs for men and boys) and assumes a fictional role, such as horse farmer or Methodist preacher. Staff members play along, remaining steadfastly in character—mention the word *airplane,* for instance, and you'll be met with a confused stare.

Home base for weekenders is a green-shuttered Victorian farmhouse where the bedrooms have oil lamps and ceramic washbasins. The chore chart is plenty long: there are likely to be fields to hoe, stables to muck, cows to milk, and eggs to gather. Still, there's plenty of time to notice that lima-bean blossoms smell like lily of the valley, and to ogle the 400-pound boar. And kids get to sample frontier education, dipping pens into inkwells in a one-room school.

Days end with a bountiful meal that might include chicken fricassee, tomatoes from the garden, graham bread with apple butter, and warm sugar cookies. Then everyone gathers on the porch for banjo playing and riddles read aloud from a book. Enjoy the past while it lasts; the next day you'll be turning in your borrowed duds and dispatched back to the present. ✚

GUIDE, PAGE 259.

Conner Prairie's 1886 farmhouse headquarters, above. Top right: Dark and Light Brahma hens. Right: A happy time-traveler. Opposite: A morning chore.

Chicago

THE LORDS OF DOGTOWN

EVER SINCE Austro-Hungarian immigrants Emil Reichel and Sam Ladany introduced Vienna-style sausages at Chicago's 1893 World's Fair, "wieners," also known as red hots, have been the city's essential food on the go. Chicago dogs aren't just served, they're built. The frank is laid on a poppy-seed bun, then layered with condiments: yellow mustard, kryptonite-green sweet relish, nibble-sized sport peppers, and a dash of celery salt. If you want the extras—tomato wedges, a dill pickle spear, diced onion—order your pup "dragged through the garden."

When the gods are with you, you'll experience what food critic Jonathan Gold has called "a steamy thing with a snap not unlike a plucked cello string and a heavenly rush of garlicky juice." So let the wiener festspiel begin: At Superdawg Drive-In, order fully tricked-out franks through a carside squawk box. Then go high-end with one of Hot Doug's daily specials—like "saucisse de Toulouse with sauce moutarde and Bergkase cheese." After hours, hit Wiener's Circle, a fixture with a tough-talking counter crew, or its genial opposite, Murphy's Red Hots, in a mom-and-pop storefront. And don't leave town without following Wolfy's roadside sign—a 40-foot fork spearing a frank—to the Char-Polish, a perfectly seasoned all-beef sausage with crackly skin. Best in show? You choose, but be warned: these dogs bite back. ✚

GUIDE, PAGE 259.

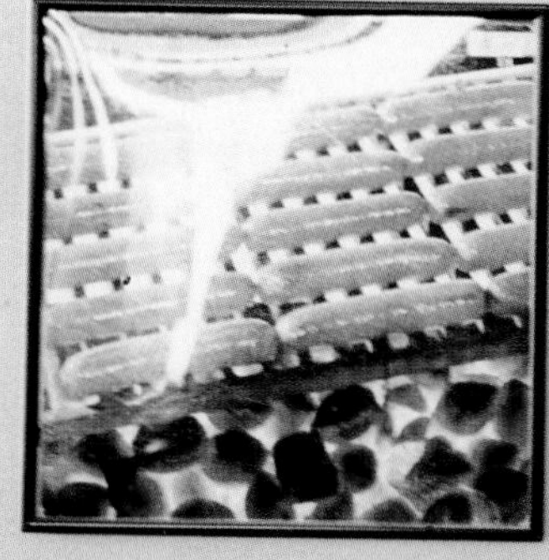

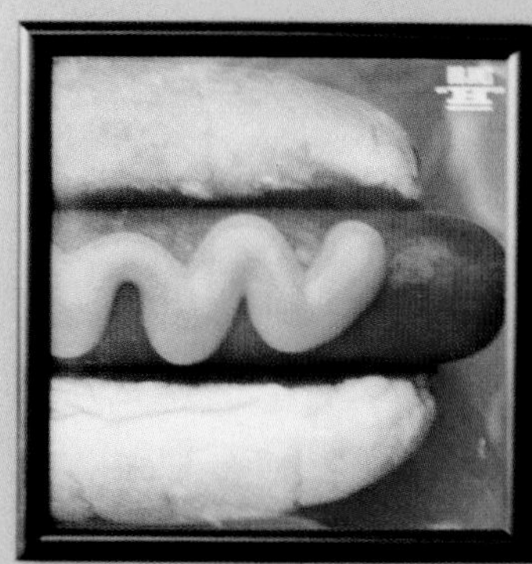

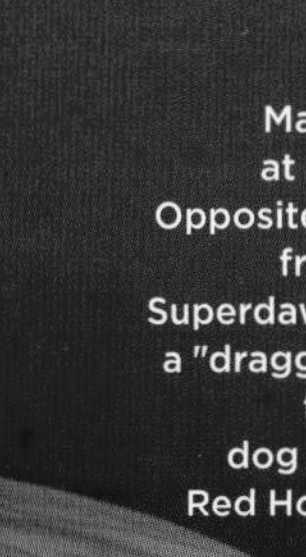

Man bites dog at Hot Doug's. Opposite, clockwise from top left: Superdawg Drive-In; a "dragged through the garden" dog at Murphy's Red Hots; Wolfy's.

Montana

AN AMERICAN INDIAN HOME ON THE RANGE

SPANISH MUSTANGS, the breed that carried thousands of Blackfeet across these plains, roam freely around Lodgepole Gallery & Tipi Village, in northwestern Montana. Blackfoot artist Darrell Norman reintroduced the light, strong equines to his people in 1994, a century after they were replaced by quarter horses. He also set up this camp: 10 canvas tepees, built and furnished as they would have been 200 years ago, facing east to welcome the sun. The gallery sells American Indian art and offers workshops where you can craft a parfleche (rawhide tote), rattle, and drum. On a tour of the flatlands, Norman shows you medicine rocks—sacred sandstone guideposts—and ancient bones embedded beneath a "buffalo jump," a cliff over which hunters drove their prey. At Glacier National Park, a few miles west, Blackfoot guides take you trout fishing and horseback riding.

For dinner, Norman and his wife cook a traditional feast of roasted buffalo, Anasazi beans, squash, and soup made from saskatoons, a blueberry-like fruit that ripens in late summer and is served at the great July Sun Dance. The evening ends with fireside singing and storytelling—and the chance to beat your own drum. ✚

GUIDE, PAGE 259.

Traditional dwellings greet the morning sun at Lodgepole Gallery & Tipi Village, in northwestern Montana.

Lakeside dining at Wynn's Bartolotta Ristorante di Mare. Opposite, from left: Bubble Bar, at Caesars Palace; the nightclub Blush, in Wynn Las Vegas.

Las Vegas

THE RED CARPET, WITHOUT THE VELVET ROPE

NO LONGER A STAGE set masquerading as a metropolis, Las Vegas has finally grown into a real global city, offering a diversity of experiences to rival any other's—from intimate to over-the-top, ersatz to authentic and (more likely) something in between. These days, Vegas is all about making the rarefied accessible—and usually more affordable. At Guy Savoy's eponymous restaurant in Paris, dinner for two will cost you $310 (that is, if you can score a table). But at the chef's convivial Bubble Bar in Caesars Palace, you can often just walk in, then sample four of his legendary creations (silky artichoke-and-truffle soup; jewel-like oysters in an icy gelée) for only $40.

Vegas specializes in this sort of nonexclusive exclusivity, making mere mortals feel like high-rolling VIPs. Celebs and hotel guests mix it up on the dance floor at Blush, the sultry nightclub at the Wynn Las Vegas, their gyrations illuminated by glowing lanterns in ever-changing hues. (Yes, that's Kobe Bryant at the corner table.) Nor does the town confine itself to big, brash, outrageous strokes. Simplicity and subtlety are on the program, too—and on the menus. At Bartolotta Ristorante di Mare, also at the Wynn, sublimely fresh fish is grilled with olive oil, lemon, and parsley, to glorious effect. The cooking is minimalist, but the décor is unabashedly maximalist: neo-Baroque chandeliers, a grand spiral staircase, and knockout views of a (fake) lake. Sometimes Vegas is still Vegas—and what's not to love? ✚

GUIDE, PAGE 259.

Vail

A SKI LEGEND GETS A BILLION-DOLLAR (FACE) LIFT

Gliding along the Sleepytime Road trail on Colorado's Vail Mountain.

VAIL IS THE BIGGEST ski mountain in the country, and has long been one of the best. But the town has always defined itself in relation to its glam rival, 96 miles down the road. Aspen is Hollywood, wild, celebutastic. Vail is Wall Street, family-oriented, with a whole lotta condos. Now that's rapidly changing.

Currently in the midst of a billion-dollar revamp, Vail—the town—has drummed up some compelling new reasons for the slope-obsessed to stick around. Among the latest lodging options inches from the mountain are the Arrabelle at Vail Square, a hotel designed as a collection of Austrian houses (with heated marble floors and ski butlers), and the Vail Plaza Hotel & Club, an Italian fantasy with balconies galore. Old-timer Tivoli Lodge is fresh from a rebuild that mixes Tyrolean coziness with Lucullan après-ski

comforts, such as Swedish walk-in showers with body jets. Ever Vail, a 9½-acre village at the base of Vail Mountain with its own main street, park, hotel, and gondola, is on track to be the nation's largest LEED-certified project for resort use. Just up the street is an in-the-works exhibition space, rumored to be a Denver Art Museum annex, and Ritz-Carlton, St. Regis, Four Seasons, and W are on their way. The whole makeover is summed up aptly by one longtime resident: "Now the town will finally equal the mountain." ✚

GUIDE, PAGE 259.

Santa Fe

SEEKING OUT A VITAL ARTS SCENE

SANTA FE'S SKIES are so wide, its altitude so giddy, that it feels like a Southwestern Shangri-la: a not-quite-real place miles above the rest of the world. A visitor might wonder how the locals came to live here, and what they find to do. Well, they write novels, plays, oratorios; they paint, photograph, sculpt. The stark beauty that drew Georgia O'Keeffe here in the 1920's still lures seekers with a creative bent, and a world-class arts scene has grown up around them.

The center of today's action is the $125 million Santa Fe Railyard, a new 50-acre complex of performance and exhibition spaces surrounding the town's historic train terminus. Site Santa Fe, a feisty nonprofit, champions cutting-edge work like Cai Guo-Qiang's dazzling installations, and James Kelly Contemporary has featured Donald Judd and Sherrie Levine. Near the Plaza—the town's hub—Robert Nichols Gallery exhibits Diego Romero's pottery, painted with Native American-inspired vignettes.

Ready for a history break? Check out the Museum of Spanish Colonial Art's conquistador furniture. Then head to Seret & Sons, an emporium of textiles and Tibetan antiques founded 30-odd years ago by Ira and Sylvia Seret. They're among the many travelers who blew into town one day and never left. ✚

GUIDE, PAGE 260.

James Kelly at his gallery, left. Above: A 1950's passenger car on display in the Santa Fe Railyard. Opposite: Exotic textiles at Seret & Sons.

Phoenix

CATCH BIG-LEAGUE BALL IN SMALL-TIME PARKS

WHO NEEDS GROUNDHOGS AND robins to tell you that winter is almost over when you've got Pitchers and Catchers—the day the first baseball players report to camp to get ready for the season ahead? For fans, the start of exhibition games in late February is practically a national holiday. Throughout March, 30 Major League teams draw nearly 2 million people to intimate fields in Florida, home to the Grapefruit League, and Arizona, the Cactus League's turf.

The latter is a home run if you're trying to pull off an easy, affordable trip: seven of the nine ballparks sit close to one another in the Phoenix metropolitan area; hotel rooms are plentiful; and tickets can be snagged online for $5 to $25, or even scalped—it's legal. The Cactus League has a trip planner and ticket information on its extensive Web site, CactusLeague.com. The grass here is achingly green, the sky blazingly blue, the ball a white meteor. And it's hot—night games are a big plus. Bring your mitt and arrive early to take part in a great spring ritual: standing outside the warm-up field and scurrying after balls hit over the fence. Chances are you'll also catch an autograph. ✚

GUIDE, PAGE 260.

Chilling at a night game at Peoria Stadium, just outside of Phoenix.

On Lake Powell's Wahweap Bay.

Lake Powell

A SOUTHWESTERN HOUSEBOAT ADVENTURE

EACH SUMMER MORNING, as the red-rock cliffs start to glow, the houseboats begin their parade across Lake Powell. Gleaming vessels with spiral staircases and rooftop hot tubs pull away from marinas. Rickety old craft with names like *Dock Potato* and *Sotally Tober* slip out of their sandy coves. They're trailed by motorboats, dinghies, and Jet Skis, all looking for fun on this glorious 186-mile-long expanse of calm water.

A 2½-hour drive northeast of the Grand Canyon, Lake Powell is the centerpiece of Glen Canyon National Recreation Area, which extends from northern Arizona to southern Utah. The 1963 damming of the Colorado River to create the lake was hotly opposed and helped spark the environmental movement, but controversy hasn't kept this enchanting place from drawing 3 million visitors a year.

The lake has six marinas. If you want to rent a houseboat, Wahweap Marina, in Page, Arizona, is a fine starting point: you can fuel up, buy supplies, and get schooled. Prefer to sleep on land? Lake Powell Resort has 350 rooms, plus pools, restaurants, and water excursions. For fishing, rent a powerboat from Wahweap, or book a guide. The lake is famous for striped bass. Complete landlubbers can even explore on foot—there are miles of trails that wend through stunning slot canyons. At day's end, look upward: in the neon-free night, the stargazing is stellar. ✚

GUIDE, PAGE 260.

Culver City

A HOLLYWOOD GHOST TOWN, REINVENTED

A birchwood bench at Gregg Fleishman Studio, below. Above left: At MODAA, curator Judit Méda Fekete with her husband and son. Above right: The Kirk Douglas Theatre.

A FEW SHORT years ago, the area between Beverly Hills and Venice was an industrial wasteland where tire shops proliferated—and memories of long-gone silver-screen luminaries hovered like shadows over the sidewalks. In its big-budget heyday this stretch was MGM Studios' backyard. Greta Garbo, Joan Crawford, and Clark Gable earned their stars here—but time and sellouts eventually earned Culver City the moniker Wheel Alley.

Thankfully, L.A.'s art crowd has re-created it as a design destination that rivals Chinatown and Santa Monica in its Technicolor glory. Besides more established galleries like Blum & Poe and outsider champion Billy Shire Fine Arts, Culver City has acquired a number of new, sensationally idiosyncratic venues. The Museum of Design, Art & Architecture (MODAA) mounts exhibitions by a diverse stable of artists, from Australian Aboriginal masters to architecture photographers Julius Shulman and Juergen Nogai. At Gregg Fleishman Studio, the designer builds geometric furniture and modular play structures with Pac-Man–like lines. Denizen Design Gallery zeroes in on furniture and sculpture by Modernist-minded locals like Sami Hayek and Bernard Brucha. And the revitalized Kirk Douglas Theatre, where David Mamet recently had a premiere, is devoted to showcasing new plays. Care to stay? The 1924 Culver Hotel, six stories of brick Renaissance Revival, is where the Munchkins holed up while filming *The Wizard of Oz.* ✚

GUIDE, PAGE 260.

San Francisco

GO WEST—AND GO GREEN—FOR THE ULTIMATE URBAN ECOTOUR

AMERICA'S PREMIER GREEN METROPOLIS has more trees, more solar power, more of everything environmentally friendly—and fewer plastic shopping bags (banned last winter). And according to Mayor Gavin Newsom, his city's values are attracting an astonishing number of visitors. Wait—people come to San Francisco not to ride the cable cars, but because their souvenirs won't be packed in nonbiodegradable petroleum derivatives? Exactly. Check into the Orchard Garden Hotel, built from concrete made of recycled fly ash and sustainably harvested wood, the first >>

The living roof of the Renzo Piano-designed California Academy of Sciences, in San Francisco's Golden Gate Park.

property in America to receive the LEED designation. No sacrifice here: the guest rooms—all pale wood and leaf patterns—are lovely. Next, head to Golden Gate Park's De Young Museum, a building clad in perforated (recycled) copper that provides shade while admitting daylight. The café serves food grown within 150 miles. The art collection is expansive, and from the 144-foot-tall observation deck, you can take in the entire town. Gaze east for a view of the Academy of Sciences, also in the park: its undulating roof is planted with beach strawberries, lupine, and California poppies.

At the south end of town is S.F. Recycling & Disposal Inc., home to a sculpture garden where castoffs have been transformed into masterpieces by a series of artists-in-residence. This dump is so downright utopian, it even supplies compost to vineyards—which, in return, supply the wine for art openings.

Of course, the most satisfying thing a values-oriented tourist (or anyone, for that matter) can do in San Francisco is eat. There are places with a defined purpose, such as Farmer Brown, a soul food restaurant in the Tenderloin dedicated to supporting African-American organic farmers, and Yield, a small bar established to promote organic and biodynamic wines. And only in San Francisco will you find an entire chain—Café Gratitude—specializing in raw vegan cuisine. Its food is unaccountably delicious.

Your tour of harbingers of a verdant future is not complete without Bayview's Flora Grubb Gardens nursery. The 72 photovoltaic panels on the roof fill the building with light, the foundation is engineered to float if the ground liquefies in an earthquake, and the solar-powered espresso machine at the café keeps running no matter what. How 21st-century is that? ✚

GUIDE, PAGE 260.

T+L Tip

EV Rental, the country's first green-minded car-rental agency, has locations at San Francisco International and San Jose International airports. Choose from among its fleet of electric, natural gas, and hybrid vehicles.

The Flora Grubb Gardens store and café, in Bayview. Opposite, from far left: Artist Scott Oliver at S.F. Recycling & Disposal Inc.; a salad at the Berkeley branch of Café Gratitude, San Francisco's vegan chain.

A view across the Willamette River. Opposite, from left: Ace Hotel's retro-chic business lounge; Ace's Room No. 308, painted by local artist Scrappers.

Portland

MAKING THE SCENE IN AMERICA'S INDIE CAPITAL

On summer nights, when the air is soft and sweet-smelling, you could be fooled into thinking Portland has always pushed an eco-utopian agenda. Walking where the light from streetlamps is dappled by coniferous trees, you'll pass green buildings, fair-trade shops, and, every few feet, solar-powered curbside meters that reject your money at times when parking is free. But stay awhile—close a few bars in the Belmont district, or chat with some punks playing hackysack downtown, and you'll learn that Portland is also a perverse and obstinate place: underneath its crunchy exterior are the living relics of a once-booming logging town that never went bust. It's this side of Portland, honest and funky and more than a little weird, that's made the town a magnetic dot on the indie circuit, drawing writers (Chuck Palahniuk), filmmakers (Gus Van Sant), and multitudes of now mainstream bands (the Dandy Warhols, the Shins, and the Decemberists, to name a few).

Burnside Street and the Willamette River form a cross that divides the city into quadrants. In Northeast, on rapidly gentrifying Alberta Street, frugal collectors and just plain gawkers saunter along the Last Thursday art walk, a monthly curbside display of underground crafts, and the local answer to established galleries' traditional First Thursdays. Then everyone heads for drinks to the Alibi, where blue-collars and creatives collide in rooms dripping with tiki kitsch. Southeast encompasses >>

T+L Tip
In "Fareless Square," an area that encompasses most of downtown Portland, rides on the public buses, streetcars, and light-rail trains are free. For a map, visit trimet.org.

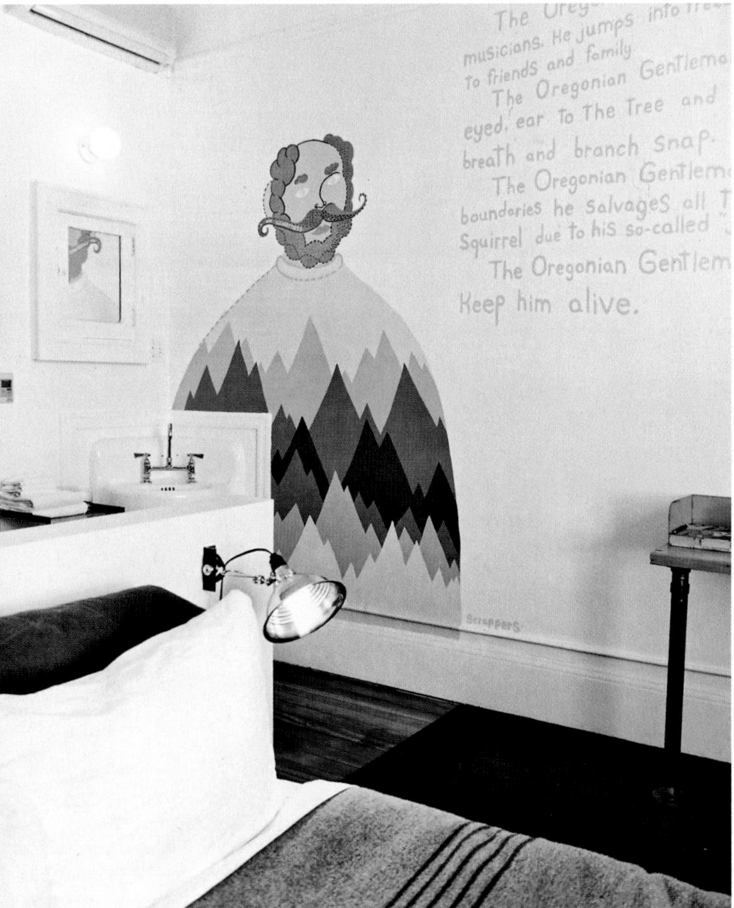

The MarchFourth Marching Band at the Doug Fir Lounge, in Southeast. Opposite, clockwise from top left: Taking a break at Burnside Skate Park; Heavenly Falls in the Japanese Garden; Southwest's South Park Blocks; organic fair-trade candies at Alma Chocolate, in Northeast.

let's-do-the-1968-time-warp Hawthorne Street (head shops, clipboard-wielding Socialists), Reed College, graffiti-scrawled Burnside Skatepark, and the log-lined Doug Fir Lounge, where you can sometimes catch the raucous MarchFourth Marching Band in their flapper-costumed, stilt-walking ensembles. Northwest starts out urban and gritty—Chinatown, Old Town—then softens into the monied calm of the Pearl District and Nob Hill. Southwest begins as a rough-and-ready nightclub zone around Mary's Club, a famed circa-1954 strip joint, before giving way to downtown offices, elm-filled park blocks, and the Japanese Garden, tranquil as any monastery's. Some of Stumptown's hipster bastions are in this quadrant: Voodoo Doughnut, where the flavors range from bacon-topped maple to vanilla-grape, and the Ace Hotel, a mod nest with murals by local and international artists.

Fashion fanatics—pierced-and-fierce pretenders to the throne of Kurt Cobain, neo-mods, gloom-and-doom girls working an emo-lite look—join the crowd at Pioneer Courthouse Square, the city's living room, which also happens to be a prime milling area for tourists. As you'll discover, it's easy to feel cool in Portland, and the old energy still resounds throughout the city, like the crack of falling timber. ✚

GUIDE, PAGE 261.

Paia

KICK BACK AND RELAX—MAUI STYLE

VIBRANT AND unpolished, this one-stoplight town on Maui's breezy north shore hasn't changed since the days when King Sugar ruled the island. Low-slung storefronts selling board shorts and the world's best fish tacos line Hana Highway and Baldwin Avenue, the main drags that meet in the center of town. Home to California escapees and an international mix of year-round beach bums, Paia (pronounced pa-*ee*-a) has lately become a windsurfing mecca—with a serious celebrity quotient. Big-wave surfing legend Laird Hamilton holds court at Anthony's Coffee Co., where the giant pancakes come with a pitcher of coconut syrup. Another beloved gathering place is Mama's Fish House, a 34-year-old, eternally packed restaurant known for its just-caught opakapaka and opah, cooked Tahitian-style. (In its backyard, right on Kuau Cove, Mama's has a little-known cluster of rental cottages that are among the few places to stay in this nearly hotel-free part of Maui.) Paia's two other chief hangouts are Mana Foods, stocked with local strawberry papayas and all manner of healthful fare, and Baldwin Beach Park, just east of the town center, where everyone boogie-boards and holds sunset barbecues.

To catch a glimpse of Hamilton and his crew slingshotting into 60-foot waves, grab your binoculars and drive just north of Hookipa Beach Park, to the cliffs that overlook the break called Jaws. In the park itself, you can watch wave-jumping and kite surfing, and explore the tide pools at your feet. Sound enticing? Pull on some surf trunks and rubber slippahs, as flip-flops are known in these parts, and you'll fit right in. ✚

GUIDE, PAGE 261.

Surfboard rentals on the Hana Highway, in Paia, above. Above left: A sorbet sundae at Mama's Fish House. Opposite: An outrigger canoe at Kuau Cove.

Kauai

HAWAII'S WILD YESTERDAY

WHAT YOU HEAR over and over on Kauai, the 550-square-mile Eden northwest of Oahu, is that this is what Hawaii looked like 30 or 40 years ago—before the high-rises, malls, fast food, and Disneyfied luaus. Oh, sure, some of that stuff is here (this is America, after all), but Kauai is so lightly touched, you can't help feeling blessed for having arrived (for once!) at a place so...before. It calls itself the Garden Island, which sounds like empty brochure-speak but is absolutely and spectacularly true. Passion vines scramble over ficus trees and bougainvillea splashes the walls of houses like flung paint.

In the northwest, the Napali Coast offers secluded beaches, reached by the incredibly muddy Kalalau Trail, rising and falling as it clings to green cliffs that plunge into the sea. Snorkel the reef off Puu Poa—crystal water with schools of fish that arrive in colored waves. Kayak up the Wailua River into a tributary edged with banyans and carpets of fern. On Kauai's south side, try the zip-line safari—a Tarzan swoop across Kipu Falls. You'll be as unbelievable as everything else on this isle: flying like a bird, and screaming like an idiot—an ecstatic idiot. ✚

GUIDE, PAGE 261.

An El Camino sporting Hawaiian shirt-inspired artwork. Opposite, from far left: Kauai's Napali Coast; a pineapple-in-progress, growing at the Hyatt Regency Kauai.

Canoeing on Lake Massawippi. Opposite, from left: One of the 41 rooms at Manoir Hovey; the inn's 1898 façade.

North Hatley

LAKE LIVING IN SMALL-TOWN QUEBEC

THE VILLAGE of North Hatley, 87 miles east of Montreal, is the summer destination of the province's heavy hitters—the premier of Quebec has a second home here. And for centuries, its main attraction, Lake Massawippi, has drawn visitors from across the border as well. More than a few of the area's stone mansions and sprawling cedar-shingled retreats were built by Southern aristocrats who began vacationing here in the late 19th-century.

The lake's deep, dark waters are perfect for swimming, fishing, canoeing, and windsurfing. You can also tour them with guide Captain Ross in his 1957 mahogany boat, *Old Shep,* which docks at the local inn of choice, Manoir Hovey, a plantation-style spread built by an Atlanta industrialist in 1898. It has 41 individually appointed rooms, many with fireplaces and lake views, and a Québécois restaurant serving treats like seared duck and pumpkin confit and the pick of a 12,000-bottle wine cellar.

There's more thought for food on Saturdays, when the town chefs gather at the farmers' market on Rue School to stock up on Bibb lettuce, lavender honey, and smoked trout. And at nearby St. Benoît-du-Lac, a Benedictine monastery, guests are invited to pick apples in the orchard and sample the house-made cider. Burn off the weekend calories on a bicycle: ride through the woods and across the covered bridges that surround the lake, or pedal off on a leg of the Route Verte, Quebec's extensive bikeway network—its Grandes-Fourches route passes right through North Hatley. ✚

GUIDE, PAGE 261.

T+L Tip

For delicious Québécois cheeses, stop by LeBaron Grocery, in the center of the village. The shop has been owned and operated by the same family since it opened in 1888.

Montreal

DESIGNING CANADIANS

NORTH AMERICA'S City of Light has made the jump from historic to hot, with a slew of stylish hotels, shops, and restaurants. Here, even laundromats compete for inspired design awards, in the aptly named contest Créativité Montréal.

For the best of the new, go straight to the Old City. Horse-drawn calèches rumble over cobblestones past such of-the-moment spots as Hôtel Gault, a 30-room hideaway outfitted with Bertoia chairs, Eileen Gray side tables, and Tolomeo lamps, and housed in an 18th-century former carpet factory.

Hit the city's contemporary-art hub in the neighborhood of Ste.-Catherine. The Belgo Building, which also once did time as a factory, now bustles with more than 30 ateliers and galleries. In the residential Plateau district, Couleurs Meubles et Objéts du 20e Siècle features an impressively edited array of Midcentury housewares. Philippe Dubuc sells its own line of slim-fitting men's suits.

After dark, head to Rue St.-Laurent's low-lit Bílý Kůň for local microbrews, or Pop! Bar à Vin, a Danish Modern nook that serves dozens of wines by the glass. At Joe Beef, in the Petit-Bourgogne, the Québécois menu (boudin, foie gras), décor (mounted bison head), and staff (tattooed master oyster shucker) exemplify the town: tradition-based, with an irreverent touch. ✚

GUIDE, PAGE 261.

Co-owner Alison Cunningham at Joe Beef, in Petit-Bourgogne, above. Left: The lobby at Hôtel Gault. Opposite: Downtown at dusk.

Hitting the class-five rapids of the Chilko River. Opposite, from left: An angler heads for the lake; yoga on the resort's private dock.

Chilko Lake

WHITE WATER AND WHITE LINENS IN THE CASCADES

TO GET TO CHILKO LAKE, you fly north from Vancouver in a private plane, over waterfalls, staggering peaks, and pine forests that seem to have no end. The lake itself is 55 miles long and 1,000 feet deep, and is buried in the mountains that Americans call the Cascades and Canadians call the Coastal Range. Here, in this magnificent isolation, is the Lodge at Chilko Lake, a rambling waterfront compound of antiques-filled log cabins and timber-frame cottages. The resident yoga instructor leads meditations and asanas on the sun-silvered dock. The chef whips up robust family-style dinners featuring wild game, local seafood, and herbs plucked from the greenhouse. The wine cellar is stocked with Pacific Northwest bottles, and cocktails can be served up over 10,000-year-old glacial ice.

But it is adventure that is the primary draw here. People come to hike mountain ridges accessible only by helicopter; to kayak across the lake, watching the silhouettes of deer shifting through the trees on the shore; to ride horses through dense woods and over golden open meadows; and, not least, to raft the class-five rapids. The Chilko River contains the longest stretch of commercially navigable white water anywhere in North America. As you shoot through the canyons, plowing through surging foam, bald eagles plunge down from the cliffs above, salmon spawn beneath you, and the bears are too busy fishing along the banks to notice your bullet-like passage. ✚

GUIDE, PAGE 261.

Lounging on the pink-sand beach at the Reefs hotel, in Bermuda.

CARIBBEAN + BERMUDA

Mangoes at a roadside fruit stand, above. Left: A Jungle Bay cottage. Opposite: Local girls in the town of La Plaine.

Dominica

WHERE THE ENVIRONMENT IS FRONT AND CENTER

As your jet descends toward the airstrip, it's easy to see why Dominica is known as one of the Caribbean's gems: 4,000-foot mountains stand verdant and craggy, 365 rivers squiggle through rain forest. Such unvarnished beauty won this former British colony the location-scout lottery, when it was cast as the main set for the *Pirates of the Caribbean* movies. Its star turn was perhaps a sign of things to come: Dominica recently deepened its port, making it navigable for jumbo cruise ships, and is spending more than $30 million to upgrade its airport. Yet even as it develops, Dominica remains authentic. Locals call nature their lifeblood and are reaching out to like-minded travelers with bicycle tours and a 118-mile hiking trail, the Waitukubuli, which will span the entire island.

The green streak runs deepest in the island's hotels. At 3 Rivers Eco Lodge, an encampment of four hillside bungalows, water is solar-heated and many toilets are self-composting. Guests of the mountain retreat Exotica Cottages feast on organic vegetables from the property's gardens. Jungle Bay Resort & Spa has 35 private cabins set on stilts to minimize erosion, and an open-air restaurant that donates kitchen scraps to farmers for fertilizer. Such good vibes (and a massage center) lure devotees of healing arts, yoga, and tai chi. Follow them to a place where your carbon footprints will be light. ✚

GUIDE, PAGE 263.

A guest room at the Montpelier Plantation Inn. Opposite, from top to bottom: Outside the Four Seasons Resort's spa; a Four Seasons villa pool.

Nevis

SMALL IS BEAUTIFUL

DON'T EXPECT mega-resorts on Nevis. This little island hasn't even got a traffic light. That's not to say it's untouched, but it has been handled with care. Rain forest still blankets much of the interior, and the shore is pristine. On the slopes of 3,200-foot Mount Nevis, old sugar plantations survive as elegant inns. The silvery sands of Pinney's Beach, on the isle's tranquil west coast, are home to the Four Seasons Resort Nevis, which devotees call the nicest retreat in the Caribbean. It's certainly this island's most luxurious, with an open-air spa (try the salt-mango scrub), a lively children's program, and stellar service: mention to your waiter that you don't like cilantro, and not a sprig will mar your plate your entire stay. The Montpelier Plantation Inn, a former sugar estate, has 17 cottage suites that are at once simple and refined.

It's a grand place to do nothing in, but even better to explore. Historic Charlestown's broad streets are lined with stone buildings dating back to the days when Victoria was queen and sugar was king. Alexander Hamilton was born here; his handsome Georgian house is now the Museum of Nevis History, which chronicles the history of locals, from early Carib Indians to the small groups of Jewish settlers who arrived in the 17th century from Brazil.

Come in late July, when Nevis celebrates its independence from England with the annual Culturama festival. The entire island turns out for a two-week carnival and lots of lymin'—that's local for *relaxing*. ✚

GUIDE, PAGE 263.

A view of Saba's capital, the Bottom. Opposite, from left: Locals kicking back in Windwardside, Saba's second-largest town; fried tiger prawns with wasabi at Queen's Gardens Resort.

Saba

A HAVEN FOR HIKERS AND BIKERS

THE ISLAND OF SABA (pronounced say-ba) is little more than a five-square-mile dormant volcano crisscrossed by a single thin, winding road. Cottages with red-tile roofs cling to precipitous slopes. And all along the coast, jagged cliffs plummet to the turquoise sea. Virtually sand-free, Saba doesn't attract beach-minded vacationers. But the Dutch-governed island (part of the Netherlands Antilles) is one of the best-preserved natural areas in the Caribbean, with tropical reefs that lure scuba enthusiasts.

The island's perimeter is protected by Saba Marine Park, with more than two dozen sites of varying depth and difficulty. Divers can watch hawksbill turtles playfully zipping between underwater pinnacles and blue trumpetfish lingering among bright corals. Even timid seahorses are regularly spotted.

Land explorers can hike a lush, forested trail up 2,855-foot Mount Scenery, the highest point in the Kingdom of the Netherlands, overlooking the Bottom, the island's principal settlement, nestled into the bowl of the volcano's caldera. Ask a local about the less strenuous—and even more scenic—Sandy Cruz trail, a rambling four-hour round-trip through groves of banana trees, with views of the shining blue waters below.

Rest up from your adventures in a crisp, whitewashed room at the Queen's Gardens Resort, the most luxurious place to stay on the island. You won't leave nature behind: lolling by the pool or dipping into the restaurant's Asian-Caribbean cooking, you'll always be within sight of Saba's beguiling sea. ✚

GUIDE, PAGE 263.

St. John

THE WILD SIDE OF THE VIRGIN ISLANDS

When Laurance Rockefeller donated 5,000 acres of prime St. John jungle and coastline to the United States government in 1956, he saved two-thirds of the island from being developed, and put Virgin Islands National Park—one of the most stunning tropical spots anywhere—forever on the map. The isle is the least populated and most pristine of the U.S. Virgin Islands, and only a 20-minute ferry ride east from crowded St. Thomas.

Rent a car in Cruz Bay, St. John's harbor town, and make the five-minute drive to the private estate-turned-hotel Caneel Bay, another Rockefeller legacy and one of the world's first

eco-resorts (opened in 1956). Wild donkeys share the grounds with guests, and the plush, low-lying bungalows are built with native woods and stones. Seven private beaches edge the grounds, and over at the Self Centre, there are guided meditation classes, couples' astrology sessions, and acupressure treatments enhanced with healing colors and sounds.

Energized? Trunk Bay, one of the Caribbean's most photographed beaches, is a quick four-wheel drive away. Grab your fins and hit the 225-yard snorkeling trail managed by the National Park Service, with plaques on the ocean floor identifying the fan-like coral sea whips, parrotfish, eels, barracuda, and blue tangs you're likely to swim past.

St. John is also laced with some 20 miles of footpaths. The ranger-guided Reef Bay Hike departs from the visitor center in Cruz Bay and winds 2½ miles downhill through rain forest, past Arawak Indian petroglyphs and four ruined sugar mills, to the ocean. There, a Park Service boat will ferry you back to Cruz Bay, where Woody's Seafood Saloon awaits with crunchy conch fritters and ice-cold bottles of Caribe. ✚

GUIDE, PAGE 263.

Nazareth Lutheran Church, in Cruz Bay, above. Left: A guest room at the Caneel Bay resort. Opposite, from far left: Looking out from the Caneel Bay resort's room No. 8; an aerial view of Caneel Bay.

Eustacia Sound, seen from the Bitter End Yacht Club, left. Above: A room at the Bitter End. Opposite: Little Dix Bay's Pavillion Bar.

Virgin Gorda

SWEET SECLUSION ON A CARIBBEAN SHORE

YOU'LL HAVE TO TAKE a puddle jumper or ferry from St. Thomas or Tortola to reach this easterly British Virgin Island. Though home to the BVI's top resorts, Virgin Gorda is blissfully un-sceney and has swaths of empty beach. Much of it is protected, giving the island a wonderfully remote, deserted feel—and many corners for quiet contemplation.

At Little Dix Bay, built by Laurance Rockefeller in the 1960's beside one of the island's prettiest shores, the rooms have exposed-rock walls, and the spa offers cliffside massages and an infinity pool. On Berchers Bay, Biras Creek Resort is perfect for solitude seekers. Or lodge in a tree-house-like beachfront villa at the sporty Bitter End Yacht Club, where you can try out all manner of small craft, from sailboards to Boston Whalers.

Virgin Gorda has few drivable roads and is best explored by boat—your resort can charter one for you. Visit the Baths, a string of small coves with half-submerged granite boulders, like marbles tossed into the sea. In Spanish Town's Yacht Harbour, shop Buck's Market for picnic goods and Thee Artistic Gallery for shell earrings and shipwreck coins.

Dress up for line-caught swordfish at Little Dix's Sugar Mill. As the hotel's steel band plays on, end your evening dancing barefoot in the sand. ✚

GUIDE, PAGE 263.

Puerto Rico

THE OTHER HALF OF PARADISE

A surfer in Rincón, on Puerto Rico's west coast, above. Above left: Guadalupe Cathedral, in Ponce. Opposite: Room No. 5 at Horned Dorset Primavera.

PUERTO RICO's western half is miles away from the bustle of San Juan: life moves slowly here, and the rhythms of tradition lie closer to the surface. Instead of discos, casinos, and mega-resorts, there are coffee plantations, seaside cafés, and midnight swims.

Begin a loop through this "other side" of the island in Mayagüez, on the central west coast. The Ruta Panorámica, 165 miles of switchbacks, starts here and ends at the island's lower east shore. This spine links hill towns, forest preserves, and historic paradors, which receive few out-of-towners. The only busy season is summer, when Puerto Rican families head to the interior highlands to escape the heat, splashing under waterfalls and hiking through woods carpeted with impatiens.

A good resting point along the route is Hacienda Gripiñas, in the island's center. Built in 1858 as the homestead of a coffee grower, the house is surrounded by gardens and the coffee plantation, which supplies the beans for the guests' morning brew. Just up the hill is the Reserva Forestal Toro Negro, more remote and untrammeled than El Yunque, San Juan's nearest jungle reserve. Book a daylong hike, with stops for ziplining and climbing up cascades, with Acampa Nature Adventures.

Continue due south to Ponce, Puerto Rico's second-largest city. Founded in the late 1600's, it enjoyed a commercial boom two centuries later—followed by a dramatic decline. For decades, its wedding-cake mansions were left to crumble. >>

A view near the Hacienda Gripiñas, off the Ruta Panorámica, left. Opposite, clockwise from top left: Horned Dorset Primavera's mango tart; a street scene in Mayagüez; Karina Moul, a resident of Rincón; a mansion in Ponce.

T+L Tip
Rincón Surf School offers lessons that fit any time-table or skill level, from two-hour introductory work-shops to five-day intensive camps.

Today, many have been restored, and the center of town is a parade of Spanish colonial balconies, balustrades, and bas-reliefs. Have lunch at Mark's at the Melia, where steak house favorites are served alongside local dishes like shrimp *mofongo:* plantains smothered in creole sauce.

West of Ponce the climate turns arid. The 10,000-acre Guánica Dry Forest harbors crested toads, purple land crabs, and a 700-year-old guayacan tree. From the tiny fishing village of La Parguera nearby, you can take a boat to a bioluminescent bay—and dive in. Further north, in the surf town of Rincón, sits what is arguably the island's most lavish hotel, the Horned Dorset Primavera, built on seven hilly acres that tumble right down to the Caribbean. The marble-floored rooms are outfitted with Balinese furniture and Moroccan lamps, and each has its own plunge pool. Meals at the restaurant are refreshingly unpretentious, served in a small cobalt-tiled dining room or on a terrace by the sea. Try the roasted deep-sea grouper.

Surfers found their way to Rincón after the World Championship here in 1968, but the town never grew too big or lost its flavor. When the sea starts churning, head-high waves curl themselves into tubes at the break line, and the town's longboard elite get down to business. Start talking to the *americanos* around here and you'll find that many have been returning for years and years. They come to ride the surf, relax on uncrowded beaches, snorkel, spot humpback whales, and cruise along twisting, turning seaside Route 413, also known—rightly—as the Road to Happiness. ✚

GUIDE, PAGE 263.

SE
ALQUILA

Nadja Talevi, a concierge, and Richard Quinn, general manager, at Cambridge Beaches. Opposite, from left: Horseshoe Bay, one of the island's most famous strands; the balcony of an Elbow Beach Spa suite.

Bermuda

A BASTION OF POLITESSE LETS LOOSE

BERMUDA'S CLEAR WATERS and high-service hotels were, until recently, largely the haunts of wealthy honeymooners and golfers. The 21-square-mile British dependency, a mere two hours by plane from New York, is far more affordable these days, thanks to the 2006 arrival of JetBlue, which forced all other airlines to come down in price. With a fresh influx of tourists, this supremely English island is bouncing back from its battering by Hurricane Fabian in 2003—and unbuttoning. At Cambridge Beaches, that poshest of old-line resorts, a colony of freshly remodeled bungalows rings a glam new multitiered infinity pool, and a romance concierge orchestrates spur-of-the-moment marriage proposals. Since Mandarin Oriental took over in 2000, grande dame Elbow Beach has shed its pink florals in favor of butter-yellow walls, blond wood, and wicker, and added a spa with hand-carved granite soaking tubs.

Even more astonishing for an island that hasn't seen a hotel open in 35 years: at least three large-scale complexes are in the works, including the Jumeirah Southlands Resort, an assembly of glass-walled suites on 37 acres of south-shore beachfront. And in the capital city of Hamilton, the old purveyors of Shetland sweaters and linen handkerchiefs have new neighbors selling Jimmy Choos and board shorts. Still, Bermuda hasn't entirely turned its back on tradition. Afternoon tea is served promptly at 4 p.m., and every August, the island takes a two-day holiday for the biggest cricket match of the year. Bermuda shorts are optional. ✚

GUIDE, PAGE 263.

Plaza de Santa Teresa, looking onto the illuminated dome of the 17th-century Convento de San Pedro Claver, in Cartagena, Colombia.

MEXICO + CENTRAL + SOUTH AMERICA

A walkway at Sayulita's Petit Hotel d'Hafa. Opposite, clockwise from left: Sayulita Bay; mahi-mahi tacos topped with mango salsa, at Sayulita Fish Taco; Alexis Mignot, nephew of Pachamama boutique's French owners, with his siblings and girlfriend.

Sayulita

HIGH STYLE IN A PACIFIC FISHING VILLAGE

WHEN THE FIRST American surfers arrived in the early seventies, Sayulita (26 miles up the coast from Puerto Vallarta on the Bay of Banderas) was an inaccessible fishing village. It has since grown into one of those high-low places where you can drop $1,800 on a leather-and-pearl necklace in an edgy boutique, waltz out past a Christie's real estate office, then have a superb 85-cent fish taco. Locals greet you before you greet them. You're not a gringo here. Everyone converges on the sand to toast the sunset: fishermen, their wives and children, surfers, retirees.

Sayulita's street food—flan sold at a card table; tangy marinated chicken grilled at stands along Calle José Mariscal—is safe and delicious. The village wakes up at Choco Banana, on the zocalo, with breakfast burritos and surfer-watching. Sayulita Fish Taco's batter-fried mahi-mahi in handmade tortillas with pineapple-mango salsa is so crazy-good, no one cares that it costs nearly $2.

For accommodations, you can rent Les Oiseaux Volants, an airy seven-bedroom duplex, whitewashed and thatched, set over the chic Pachamama boutique. Or check into the Petit Hotel d'Hafa, a Moroccan whimsy with pierced-tin wall lamps and straw mats stenciled in flowers and crescent moons. ✚

GUIDE, PAGE 265.

Monarch butterflies migrating through Michoacán's El Rosario sanctuary.

Michoacán

FOLLOW THE BUTTERFLIES TO THE MEXICAN COAST

ON PAPER-THIN WINGS they fly from as far north as Canada to Mexico's Sierra Madre Occidental. Most monarch butterflies live only two to six weeks, but, for reasons scientists don't fully understand, the season's last brood survives up to eight months—long enough to make the arduous trip south. Every fall, they arrive by the millions to hibernate and mate in 217 square miles of nature reserves. During peak season—February and March—visitors can witness this migration in fir groves where monarchs cover trees in pulsating cloaks of orange and onyx.

The two best preserves are El Rosario and Sierra Chincua, on the eastern edge of Michoacán state. Each is a 45-minute drive from Angangueo, a historic mining town that's the unofficial capital of monarch country. El Rosario's easy, mile-long hiking path leads right into the thick of things; Sierra Chincua visitors can rent horses for a trek into viewing areas. Both tours are guided by local farmers. Go just after noon, when the sun warms the butterflies awake and the beating of wings sounds like the rumble of a distant waterfall. ✚

GUIDE, PAGE 265.

T+L Tip

The World Wildlife Fund posts information about the butterfly sanctuaries, with driving directions, at wwf.org.mx.

Oaxaca

A BELOVED CITY RISES AGAIN

WITH ITS WELL-PRESERVED 17th-century architecture, intriguing food (flash-fried grasshoppers, 20-ingredient moles), and thriving crafts markets, Oaxaca has long been a favorite stop on the Mexico travelers' circuit. But after a series of political protests landed the city in newspapers around the world in 2006, many visitors simply stopped coming, and the destination became oddly quiet.

Now Oaxaca is waking up again, and it's an opportune time to stroll its cobblestoned streets and linger at the open-air cafés ringing the zocalo. The plaza, dotted with 100-year-old laurel trees, serves as the city's social and economic heart, and is as magnificent as ever. So are the imposing Baroque cathedral, which sits on the square's western edge, and the ornately decorated colonial church of Santo Domingo, a few blocks north.

The Camino Real Hotel, a converted convent, still has the city's loveliest lodgings. Its 16th-century frescoes, bougainvillea-draped courtyards, and massive octagonal fountain survived the political turmoil intact.

Oaxaca is, of course, also the gateway to a host of traditional artisans' villages, as well as to archaeological sites such as Monte Albán, ancient capital of the Zapotec. The forests and peaks of the Sierra Norte are less than 40 miles away.

As if the city itself, with its dynamic living history continually unfolding, wasn't reason enough to visit. ✚

GUIDE, PAGE 265.

A religious procession in Teotitlán del Valle, a traditional carpet-weaving village near the city of Oaxaca. Opposite, from far left: A room at the Camino Real Hotel; outside Oaxaca's 1572 Santo Domingo Church.

Riviera Maya

IN THE YUCATÁN, A FAMILY-FRIENDLY RETREAT

THE YUCATÁN peninsula's eastern shore, a quick drive south of Cancún, is home to spectacular beaches, Mayan ruins, and the world's second-longest coral reef. For years a hideout for hippies and honeymooners, the Riviera Maya is now a magnet for families, thanks to its wide range of waterfront resorts, and two dreamy options in particular. Parents seeking tranquility stay at the Hotel Esencia, with 29 all-white rooms and suites, an organic spa, and one of the area's top restaurants. Kids get their own yoga sessions and cacao bean-oil "chocolate" massages. Those looking for a bit more action will prefer the Azul Beach Hotel, an all-inclusive with a kids' club and a surprisingly hip vibe.

Wherever you hang your hat, be sure to get out and explore. The white stone ruins of Tulum—surrounded by manicured lawns on a bluff overlooking the Caribbean—are among the best maintained and most visually striking of ancient Mayan sites. Looking for a surreal snorkeling spot? The Yucatán coast is dotted with thousands of cenotes, limestone sinkholes with freshwater pools that served the Maya as entrances to mysterious underground river systems; local outfit Hidden Worlds conducts guided excursions.

Xcaret and Xel-Ha are two environmentally friendly and exceptionally fun water parks. Each has an outdoor interactive aquarium where you can actually swim with parrot fish and manta rays. In the evening, Xcaret presents dazzling reenactments of Meso-American Indian games, complete with costumes and balls of fire. ✚

GUIDE, PAGE 265.

Chaise longues beside the Azul Beach Hotel's adult pool, right. Above, from left: A snorkeler; guests in a suite at Hotel Esencia. Opposite: A view of the Tulum ruins overlooking the beach.

On a terrace at Harmony Hotel. Opposite, from left: In the surf at Playa Guiones; water lilies on a Nosara pond.

Nosara

A LAID-BACK SURFERS' HIDEOUT

T+L Tip
For guided wildlife-watching and angling trips on the nearby Rio Nosara and Rio Montana, contact Nosara Boat Tours.

IN A COUNTRY THAT DRAWS legions of nomads in search of soft sands and wild surf, Nosara remains delightfully uncluttered. Built on a wide-open stretch of the Nicoya Peninsula (part of Costa Rica's Pacific coast), this tiny village has long been a haunt of surfers and other hardy souls who are happy to play in the roaring waves all day and crash in hammocks at night. Iguanas sunbathe on the main road into town; howler monkeys bellow from the surrounding forest canopy.

Lately, however, a clutch of graceful accommodations has raised the comfort bar, without overshadowing the area's untamed beauty. A bumpy dirt track leads to the Harmony Hotel, a 24-room property so environmentally minded, it employs an on-site "sustainability coordinator." In the morning, take the path through the banana trees to Playa Guiones, a four-mile-long strip where surfers find some of Costa Rica's most consistent waves. Spend the afternoon de-stressing at the yoga studio, and the evening lingering over black beans and local red snapper at the open-air restaurant.

On Nosara's northern edge, the attentively run, six-room Hotel Lagarta Lodge overlooks a 90-acre biological reserve, where guests are invited to hike myriad trails. Hotel staff can also arrange for you to tour the mangroves in a silent-running electric boat—the better to observe crocodiles asleep on the banks.

During the rainy season, May to November, you can witness an awesome spectacle: thousands of Olive Ridley sea turtles coming ashore to lay their eggs under the full moon. Nosara receives the steadiest sunshine from December to April, but its rich wildlife is on display all year. ✚

GUIDE, PAGE 265.

Cartagena

LATIN AMERICA'S LATEST HOTSPOT

VISITING CARTAGENA, an old walled seaport on Colombia's northwest coast, is like joining a cabal of travelers who could spend a week anywhere in the world but come here for a dash of jet-set flash—and a potential Gabriel García Márquez sighting. (The author is a part-time resident.) It's one of the prettiest cities around: Imagine Havana with a fraction of the population, San Juan unmodernized, New Orleans without sophomores on spring break. And it's only a 2½-hour flight from Miami.

Founded in 1533, Cartagena was exceptionally wealthy by the early 1700's, thanks to an economy of gold, sugar, and slavery. Exquisite stucco mansions with terra-cotta roof tiles are a legacy of that prosperous period, and a handful of them have lately been turned into hotels. Hotel Agua's six light-filled bedrooms are decorated with locally made woven-rush furnishings. Casa Pestagua's stately chambers offer 20-foot-tall frescoed walls and 19th-century antiques smelling of beeswax. At the grand Hotel Charleston Cartagena, set in the 300-year-old cloister of Santa Teresa, balconies overlook the sea and a Modernist spa.

Cartagena's restaurants match up. At 8-18, braised *rabo de toro,* or oxtail, with mashed potatoes is a perennial favorite. Loftlike Palma serves refined South American classics: Try ceviche of corbina with lime, hot peppers, and corn. La Vitrola is the town's power spot, with slowly spinning ceiling fans and waiters in crisp white uniforms. Regulars wave away the menu and order the grilled fish of the day.

Getsemaní, a working-class area barely touched by Cartagena's renaissance, is the place to bar hop (to be safe, go by taxi). The walls at friendly Café Havana are covered with black-and-white photos of Celia Cruz and Ibrahim Ferrer. At Quiebra Canto, rum-fueled couples salsa out onto the balcony far into the night. ✚

GUIDE, PAGE 265.

The pool at El Marqués, a colonial house turned hotel, right. Above right: A spa room at Hotel Charleston. Opposite: Old Town, founded in 1533.

Lake Titicaca

A LOFTY ANDEAN REGION OPENS UP

FOR CENTURIES, 3,200-square-mile Lake Titicaca, which straddles the Peru-Bolivia border at the dizzying height of 12,500 feet, has been a cradle of Andean civilization. It is the mythical birthplace of the Incas, and home to the Uro, Aymara, and Quechua peoples. But infrastructure for travelers has been extremely limited, and posed risks to the region's natural and cultural heritage.

Until now. Peru's most innovative and eco-minded luxury hotel company, Inkaterra, has just opened Titilaka, an 18-room lodge with such amenities as soaking tubs, radiant floor heating, and stunning lake views. Local farmers supply food for the restaurant, and excursions include guide-led visits to Titicaca's famous floating islands.

Tour operator All Ways Travel created a program on Isla Anapia that ensures islanders benefit from visitor homestays, and, thanks to UNESCO, the hand-loomed textiles of Isla Taquile's Aymara people are garnering attention. What's more, the entire region is being considered for World Heritage site status, giving Machu Picchu some friendly competition. ✚

GUIDE, PAGE 265.

An entrance arch on Isla Taquile, above. Above left: A procession of Taquileños in hand-woven fabrics. Opposite: A view from Taquile.

The dining room at the Casablanca Valley's Indòmita, above. Left: The Garcés Silva winery, in San Antonio. Opposite: A lunch of roast lamb and salad at Veramonte, in the Casablanca Valley.

Casablanca Valley and San Antonio

THE NEXT GREAT WINE COUNTRY

CHILE IS KNOWN for making $8 wines that taste as if they cost $12—something of a dubious honor. But two regions have been pushing the country's viticultural industry into a higher realm, and both can be accessed on a day trip from Santiago, the country's capital. Think of established Casablanca Valley as an aspiring Napa; nearby San Antonio, which didn't have a single vine until 1995, is its Sonoma. The landscape of the two appellations (fertile vales, forested mountains) makes for stirring drives between wineries, which you should cap with meals at the excellent vineyard restaurants, many of which only serve lunch.

At Indòmita, Oscar Tapia, one of Chile's finest chefs, dishes up a duck confit and *chilote* stew that brings out the best in the maker's full-flavored reds. Down the hill, at House of Morandé, Christopher Carpentier serves baby octopus with pisco-sour mayonnaise. The glass-walled dining room looks out onto rows of vines. The Veramonte winery puts on a charmingly rustic alfresco barbecue (among the seats: hay bales), best enjoyed with a glass of their luscious Carmenère-Merlot-Cabernet blend as you toast the future of these two rising-star regions. ✚

GUIDE, PAGE 265.

Buenos Aires

WHERE FASHION IS QUEEN

EVA PERÓN WILL ALWAYS be remembered for (among other things) her elegant wardrobe. She'd have had a field day in contemporary Buenos Aires. Argentina's style-obsessed capital is one of the world's best places to shop—and although the economy has largely recovered from the collapse of the peso in 2001, a favorable exchange rate with the dollar still makes for exceptionally good value.

Not far from where Evita is buried, in Recoleta, the boulevards are lined with Hermès and Louis Vuitton, but local labels are the draw. At Perez Sanz, the bags include a triangular purse decked in silver and rare apple-green gems. Arandú celebrates the haute-gaucho look with supple suede hunting bags and burnished riding boots.

At Plaza Dorrego's Sunday flea market, in San Telmo, stalls burst with crystal chandeliers and sterling flatware that once graced the finest *porteño* dining rooms. Radiating side streets offer an array of quirky stores. Gil Antigüedades, a vintage trove, carries one-shouldered sequined originals from Paco Jamandreu, confidant and dresser of Madame Perón herself.

The hub of this retail renaissance is leafy Palermo Viejo, where dozens of new designers have set up shop. At Mariano Toledo, a slouchy sailor-stripe shirt is paired with a pleated mini, bright floral tights, and a shiny buckled bag. Lucila Iotti, a temple to shoes, sells high-heeled patent brogues in color combos like orange and gray. Evita would undoubtedly approve. ✚

GUIDE, PAGE 265.

Inside Lucila Iotti, a shoe boutique in Buenos Aires's Palermo Viejo neighborhood, right.

Lake District

DRIVING PATAGONIA'S ALPINE WILDERNESS

ARGENTINA HAS more exotic destinations—Tierra del Fuego, the glaciers of the extreme south—but none so refreshing as the Lake District, which covers thousands of square miles in pine-covered northwestern Patagonia. Skiers come from all over to tackle the slopes in July and August (winter here) but otherwise the region is blessedly unknown to foreigners. It's a favorite escape for Argentines, who love the alpine villages and grandiose stone-and-wood lodges. Picture a band of gauchos singing "Edelweiss" by the campfire and you've got the general idea.

The region is perfect for road trips. Its gateway, San Carlos de Bariloche, is a two-hour flight from Buenos Aires; just beyond baggage claim lie rugged forests, glassy waters, and icy peaks. Stay at the Llao Llao Hotel & Resort, 20 miles north of town in a landscape of towering granite mountains crowned by glistening snow. The hotel's steep roofs, massive chimneys, and deer-antler chandeliers are equally as dramatic.

Next day, head south through Nahuel Huapi National Park and hike to the Cascada de los Césares, a 230-foot waterfall. From there, go north 100 miles on the (mostly unpaved) Route of the Seven Lakes to San Martín de los Andes, a scruffy, charming pueblo, for lunch at the Hamburgueseria Peperone. Take the trail along Juez del Valle for a view of Patagonian steppes (east) and Lake Lácar, stretching to Chile (west).

The road returns to Bariloche through a misty green valley dotted with sheep. Visit nearby Los Arrayanes National Park to see stands of centuries-old arrayán trees, with their twisted trunks and smooth, cinnamon-hued bark. Then soothe away any road-weariness with a stay at Correntoso Lake & River Hotel, a luxe fishing resort with an infinity pool and a hammam. ✚

GUIDE, PAGE 265.

Correntoso Lake & River Hotel's lobby, above. Clockwise from below: A San Martín de los Andes resident; a road-side chapel. Opposite: Correntoso Lake & River Hotel.

The early-19th-century Pont St.-Pierre, spanning the Garonne River in Bordeaux, France.

WESTERN EUROPE

London

YOUNG CHEFS MAKE THE CITY SIZZLE

IT'S NOT EASY to follow the acts of megastars like Gordon Ramsay and Jamie Oliver. Yet six youthful chefs have lately leaped that culinary bar and taken London by storm. Before Mark Jankel could peek over a kitchen counter, he was cooking with his grandmother in Málaga, Spain. Today the 31-year-old keeps it local: the Jerusalem artichokes he serves with pan-fried halibut at Notting Hill Brasserie come from a neighbor's garden. He also oversees two sister eateries, the Ebury and the Waterway; his dream is to open London's first completely sustainable restaurant.

At Notting Hill's airy Ledbury, 29-year-old Aussie Brett Graham makes subtle use of Asian staples like *shiso* and soy. "I'm not into molecular gastronomy. I get bored," he says.

Brett would rather confit a suckling pig for 24 hours and garnish it with mangosteens dunked in house-made pork sauce.

Pork also gets loving treatment at Trinity, in Clapham, where Adam Byatt turns a pig's head into crisp croquettes, served in pea soup with a drizzle of lobster oil. The warm, walnut-paneled dining room is a perfect place to enjoy his hearty yet refined creations. Odette's, a once stodgy Primrose Hill institution, has been revamped. The new eye-popping but elegant interior suits the light, mod-Brit food of Bryn Williams, who draws on a Welsh childhood and French training in his signature pan-fried turbot with braised oxtail and English cockles.

Jean-Philippe Patruno was born in Marseilles, but his Fino, in Soho, was inspired by Spain. Seafood dominates the tapas-style degustation menu, highlighted by *pulpo a la Gallega* (carpaccio of boiled octopus) and clams with sherry and Iberian ham. In Mayfair, River Café veteran Theo Randall channels Italy at his temple in the InterContinental, making his pasta by hand each day. But he puts the English on it with locally sourced ingredients (native porcini, grouse) that are as much this city's culinary pride as the talents of its brilliant chefs. ✚

GUIDE, PAGE 267.

Ballotine of foie gras at the Ledbury, above. Above left: The Ledbury's chef, Brett Graham. Opposite, from far left: Pig's trotter on toast with quail eggs, at Trinity; Notting Hill Brasserie's dining room.

Brighton

A CLASSIC ENGLISH SEASIDE RESORT, REDUX

LESS THAN AN HOUR by train from London, Brighton has been a louche getaway ever since the Prince Regent and Mrs. Fitzherbert romped in the Royal Pavilion 200 years ago (the palace, which Queen Victoria sold to the town, is an orgy of chinoiserie and exoticism that makes Versailles look banal). Secret shenanigans are as much a part of the landscape as dreamy Regency townhouses. When T. S. Eliot wanted to inject a bit of moral decay into *The Waste Land,* he didn't have to look further than Brighton.

Today, visits here are in better taste. An injection of trendiness has spiffed up the city's shopping, food, and nightlife. One watershed: the 2000 debut of Blanch House, a preposterously cool boutique hotel. The dining room is *Clockwork Orange* white, hilarious in the context of this town. The bar caters to hip *Wallpaper*-reading London transplants, who've made Brighton real estate among the U.K.'s most expensive. These arrivistes have sparked a full-throttle Nigellaization of the culinary scene. Blanch House's restaurant serves cardamom fritters and Earl Grey ice cream; the gastropub Forager dishes up organic Yorkshire pudding.

Chic boutiques and galleries are found along the narrow passages known as the Lanes; the Moorish-inspired Brighton Museum's collection runs from Alma-Tadema to Frank Stella. But pockets of raffishness remain, such as the great charred skeleton of the old West Pier, like a giant Louise Bourgeois crustacean, and Kemp Town, where trannies in sequins burst proudly out of doorways. Without them, rich Brighton would be poor indeed. ✚

GUIDE, PAGE 267.

The Royal Pavilion, above. Above left: Blanch House's Restaurant. Opposite: A beachfront merry-go-round.

Liverpool

THE ARTS BEAT GOES ON IN THE BEATLES' HOMETOWN

OFF TO THE SIDE, out of the mainstream, this gussied-up sailors' town is quirky and flavorsome, and almost preternaturally insular. Liverpudlians take stubborn pride in all things local and no interest in outside opinion. If you're from Liverpool, you stay here. If you aren't, you likely won't visit, except on a Beatles pilgrimage.

That's a pity, because the birthplace of the Fab Four is a hot metropolis, named the European Capital of Culture for 2008. The Tate Liverpool and Walker Art Gallery display international masters. The Bluecoat arts center, where Yoko Ono debuted, shows avant-garde installations. The Everyman Theatre and the Liverpool Playhouse stage new and classic plays from the surrounding region and beyond. Restaurant food is steadfastly earthy, but ambitious—at London Carriage Works, chef Paul Askew hopes to earn Liverpool's first Michelin star. Yet the city never Disneyfied its biggest draw: the best Fab Four theme park is Liverpool itself, unadorned and still as rakish at heart as it was in early shots of the lads, leather-jacketed, their collars turned up against the wind. ✚

GUIDE, PAGE 267.

The restored Albert dock, on the River Mersey. Opposite, clockwise from far left: The Philharmonic Pub, on Hope Street; the Tate Liverpool; inside the Malmaison hotel.

Wales

AN AGELESS LANDSCAPE GETS A NEW GENERATION OF INNS

MISTY CAMBRIAN FOOTHILLS; oak-dotted farmland; stone bridges standing like sentinels over the River Wye. Of Wales's many attributes, 'picturesqueness' is surely the most pronounced. The country is equal parts intimate and majestic, but it has long had one unfortunate trait: a reputation for uninspired lodgings and cuisine. How times change. Today a handful of upstart inns with buzzworthy restaurants are luring travelers away from the Cotswolds and Dorset.

Among the new breed, contemporary art mingles with overstuffed English furniture, and the trappings of Welsh country living are elevated with luxurious bath products and high-thread-count sheets. In Monmouthshire, the eight-room Bell at Skenfrith, built in 1690, offers knockout views of the river and the ruins of Skenfrith Castle. For dinner, local Talgarth beef comes from the nearby butcher, and duck and game are courtesy of the ace-marksman owner. At Llys Meddyg, on the coast in Newport, the best rooms are done up in an urbane, neutral palette, with reclaimed-wood headboards and slate bathroom floors. The kitchen lets local ingredients shine with simple preparations: lamb cutlets in a rosemary jus, a subtly spiced pumpkin soup. And in Brecon, in the shadow of the Black Mountains, the seven rooms at Felin Fach Griffin mix the exotic with the familiar—antique Moroccan four-poster beds are covered in woolen blankets that are 100 percent Welsh. Meals are the very model of excellent British pub grub, and breakfast is the highlight: fresh-baked bread that you grill yourself over the Aga stove, slathered with Welsh butter and tart house-made jams. ✚

GUIDE, PAGE 267.

A guest room at the Bell at Skenfrith, top right.
Right: In the Bell at Skenfrith's dining room.
Opposite: The 11th-century Pembrokeshire Castle.

The Lowlands

FOR A SHOT OF SCOTLAND'S FINEST

WHISKY IS ARGUABLY what the world loves most about Scotland. Highlands distilleries get all the glory, but Lowlands single malts—dry, delicate, and much subtler than their knock-you-out upcountry cousins—are a perfect introduction to the drink. The region has only a handful of producers, among them Glenkinchie, outside Edinburgh, and Auchentoshan, near Glasgow (one of the few labels in Scotland using a triple distillation process, resulting in an exceptionally light and refined whisky). Both have tasting rooms.

Then there's 192-year-old Bladnoch, Scotland's southernmost distillery, set in achingly beautiful Dumfries and Galloway, where the pastoral calm of velvety, undulating hills is balanced by

a craggy coastline and dark forests of ancient trees. To visit, head for the market town of Newton Stewart, a two-hour drive from Glasgow, and check into Kirroughtree House, a stately manor-inn on whose grand staircase, legend has it, Robert Burns used to recite poetry. Bladnoch's riverside facility, just seven miles south, offers tours and tastings throughout the day.

The truly obsessed can enroll in the distillery's twice-yearly weekend Whisky School. Following the stillman on his rounds, students learn how to tell if the mash tun is draining properly into the washback (watch the texture of the foam); check the mixture for consistency (the key is a slow distillation); and ensure that the cows don't get drunk from the fermenting grain, which, after distillation, becomes their feed (carefully squeeze the mash to extract the sugar water).

Between classes there is downtime for snacking on mutton pies and lolling among the daffodils on the riverbank. Graduates can take the Burns trail to Ballantrae, in Ayrshire, and toast their success at Glenapp Castle, a 17-room sandstone hotel set in majestic gardens and filled with polished French antiques and more truffle honey and artisanal cheese than the sturdiest Scots chief could imagine. ✚

GUIDE, PAGE 267.

Inside Kirroughtree House, above. Above left: The gardens at Glenapp Castle. Opposite, from far left: A local hunter; single malt at Bladnoch Distillery; sheep near Bladnoch.

The latest crop at Ballyvolane House. Opposite, from left: Ballyvolane House's steamed globe artichoke with Irish butter sauce; Chef Robert Gleeson.

County Cork

CULINARY ADVENTURES IN IRELAND'S SOUTHWEST

DRIVE SOUTH FROM Shannon airport on gradually narrowing roads, where greenswards ripple toward cliffs that plunge into the Atlantic, and you'll find yourself...on the edge of the earth? No, at epicure central. Back in 1964, at her Ballymaloe House restaurant, in Cork City, Myrtle Allen proved that Irish farmhouse cooking could garner worldwide critical acclaim. Since then, Allen and her family have expanded their enterprise with a cooking school, more restaurants in Cork City, television shows, and many books—and West Cork has developed into a vibrant and tightly knit community of artisanal food producers.

Begin your eating adventure in Bantry at Manning's Emporium, a stand stocked with West Cork cheeses. Sample Ardrahan, Carrigaline, Coolea, Durrus, and Gubbeen. Get your cheese slice from Rory Conner, a cutler whose sought-after knives are works of art, with handles of sustainable cocobolo and Irish bog oak.

Seven miles from Bantry s picturesque port, in Durrus, you'll likely find the doors swung wide open at the Good Things Café. The saffron-spiked fish soup is chock-full of haddock and Ahakista scallops, and served with a dollop of garlicky rouille: the liquid equivalent of a sun-drenched, sea-breezy day.

Next, stop at Clonakilty, famous for Ireland's most humble victual, black pudding, a sausage >>

made of cow's blood boiled with oatmeal and spices. At Gleeson's Restaurant, it's infused with rosemary and clove, and served alongside fall-apart-tender pork belly. Cap the evening with another national treasure: a trad music session nearby at the candlelit white cottage An Teach Beag.

In bustling Cork City, hasten to the English Market, a 1780's brick pile wedged tightly into the Old Town. It's jammed with fishmongers, butchers, cheese purveyors, and *traiteurs*. The Farmgate Café, on the second-floor mezzanine, is where farmers and marketers alike tuck into lamb livers and bacon at communal tables. If only every market had a restaurant this winning.

The Irish worry that their rapidly growing economy—dubbed the Celtic Tiger—may turn fishermen into builders and pubs into mere bars. But the future of hospitality on the Emerald Isle is decidedly more promising than that. The proof is in the black pudding, but if you need more, end your trip with a stay at Ballyvolane House, within a half hour's drive of Cork. An elderflower cordial awaits next to the vintage Bakelite radio in your room, but don't linger over it too long. Grab one of the hotel's fishing permits (coveted in these parts) and a pair of waders, and head for the river, 15 minutes away. A herd of jet black cows is likely to be watching as you wait to hook your sashimi. And if all you catch is a craving for seafood, head to Moran's Oyster Cottage, outside of Galway, where the eponymous shellfish are as creamy as they ever were. ✚

GUIDE, PAGE 268.

The woods behind Glengarriff Lodge, 60 miles from Cork City, above. Above left: Ballyvolane House's Big Room. Opposite: a seafood platter at Fishy Fishy Café, in the town of Kinsale.

Andalusia

A SLOW RIDE THROUGH SOUTHERN SPAIN

THERE'S NO MORE romantic way to see Andalusia than from behind the wheel of a car. Discoveries roll by: towns with tiled courtyards, orange trees, and secret gardens; hilltops with breathtaking views.

Start in Córdoba, with its famed Mezquita, an eighth-century mosque transformed into a Baroque cathedral. From there, drive southwest to Seville, where the labyrinthine 14th-century Alcázar palace abuts lively dance bars. On Thursday evenings at El Centro Cultural Cajasol, flamenco stars sing of love lost and found. Next, visit two of the region's best "white villages." Antequera lies behind La Peña de los Enamorados, or Lovers' Rock, named centuries ago for a Christian Romeo and Muslim Juliet. Iznájar has a 1,200-year-old ruined castle perfect for exploring, and, just outside town, Casa Rural El Olivar, a bed-and-breakfast nestled among acres of olive trees. End with a stay in Granada, last seat of the rulers of Muslim Spain and site of the Alhambra, their fabulous 14th-century palace.

For sustenance along the way, try serrano suckling pig and sautéed garbanzo beans at Taberna Salinas in Córdoba, and paella at the Barceló La Bobadilla hotel, in the Loja area. Celebrate in Granada at Restaurante Ruta del Azafrán, where you'll also feast your eyes: the top tables have Alhambra views. ✚

GUIDE, PAGE 268.

At Casa Rural El Olivar, in Iznájar. Opposite, from far left: A canal by the old city walls of Córdoba; a street in Seville near the Alcázar.

San Sebastián

WHERE COOKING MET CHEMISTRY

THANKS TO the mad inventiveness of its chefs, this Basque town has a trio of Michelin three-starred restaurants—compare that with nine for all of Germany. Located on the coast of Bahía de la Concha, San Sebastián has long been known for its sublime seafood and the hyperfresh produce grown in the lush, hilly farmland that lies just beyond its borders. And in recent years this metropolis of Belle Époque architecture and medieval alleyways has become the epicenter of Spain's new-wave cuisine.

At Arzak, chef Juan Mari Arzak and his daughter Elana treat diners to rich, classic Basque flavors while smacking them upside the head with remarkable new extravaganzas such as fresh tuna in bright green cucumber sauce, and a melon ball filled with sheep's-milk cheese... and Pop Rocks. At Martín Berasategui's restaurant—one of the Michelin Three—each small plate is a knockout. Roasted Araiz pigeon comes laced with cream of lime and basil. A mille-feuille of smoked eel includes foie gras, spring onions, and green apple. Lunch lasts for hours, a hushed and contemplative marathon.

But simple eating can be just as divine. Markets sell plump fruit, crusty artisanal breads, and house-cured ham. In Getaria, a fishing village about 15 miles west of San Sebastián, the old-style family restaurant San Prudencio serves a salad of tomatoes from the garden out back. Just-caught squid is cooked in its own ink. And the white wine, a Txacoli from local grapes, is slightly effervescent: rooted in tradition, but with an unmistakably fresh sparkle. ✚

GUIDE, PAGE 268.

Arzak's "squid as a star" plate, above left. Above right: A view of Bahía de la Concha. Opposite: Father-and-daughter chefs Juan Mari and Elana Arzak.

Outside Le Pure Café. Opposite, from left: Mélac Bistrot à Vins; at Café des Deux Moulins.

Paris

THE CITY'S MOST INTIMATE CORNERS

THE FRENCH LAVISH tender feelings on their *zincs,* those working-class bistros named for the galvanized bar tops that often serve as their nerve centers. In *The Belly of Paris* (1873), Émile Zola defines *zinc* as a "counter for serving customers, in bars, cafés." By 1880, the term described the bars and cafés themselves.

You go to a Paris *zinc* to absorb the flavor of its neighborhood, its industry—and its cooking. In the 11th Arrondissement, once the quarter of typesetters and printers, the earthy Mélac Bistrot à Vins, there since 1938, serves a *farçou* (onions, lardons, and chard bound in crêpe batter) that is a revelation. Nearby is Le Pure Café, with a horseshoe-shaped bar and dishes like cuttlefish with sesame seeds. The Ninth Arrondissement's businessmen come to Le Laffitte for patriotic comfort food: duck breast with green peppercorn sauce, chocolate mousse. Café des Deux Moulins is in Montmartre; its crème brûlée starred in *Amélie,* but despite the publicity conferred by the film, the place still belongs to the quartier's shopkeepers, retirees, and *fainéants.* The habitués of a *zinc* are *chez eux*—coming and going, reading and slandering, daydreaming and grumbling. Take a seat. No one can pretend to know and love Paris and not know and love its *zincs.* ✚

GUIDE, PAGE 268.

Bordeaux

RAISING A GLASS TO VISITORS

A FRIENDLIER, MORE WELCOMING France? In Bordeaux, the country's oldest and most iconic wine-growing region, the answer is yes. Falling sales among its many bottlings (due to a large increase in worldwide production) have caused many Bordelais to embrace—not just tolerate—visitors. Once top producers here sighed when the tour group arrived; now they are gussying up their châteaus and actively courting enthusiasts, conducting animated tastings, and offering patient explanations of viticulture and classification. Suddenly, it's downright pleasant to amble through the celebrated wineries of St.-Estèphe, St.-Julien, Margaux, and Arcins, and to explore the nearby regions of St.-Émilion, Graves, and the Médoc peninsula.

It's not just the winemakers who are bringing change to the 460 square miles of vineyard-strewn countryside. A new wave of contemporary, high-style hotels and *chambres d'hôtes* has swept in. Among them are Château les Merles, featuring a nine-hole golf course on its grounds; Château Rigaud, with moody blue >>

The Pont St.-Pierre, spanning the Garonne River in the city of Bordeaux. Opposite, from far left: A waiter at Le Petit Commerce; a vineyard in St.-Émilion.

T+L Tip
The novel Vipers' Tangle, *by Nobel laureate and native Bordelais François Mauriac, makes for a perfect read as you travel the region.*

walls and its own screening room (complete with faux-fur-lined couches); and La Maison Bord'eaux, which has bright, minimalist interiors that are a chic addition to a region short on up-to-date lodging.

Not coincidentally, some of the most interesting chefs in France have also gravitated to the Bordeaux area and are creating highly technical, intellectually adventurous dishes. Château Cordeillan-Bages, an 18th-century Relais & Château property, is where chef Thierry Marx, the Gault Millau 2006 chef of the year and a local culinary ringleader, concocts chocolate-coated lamb, and apple sorbet dipped in liquid nitrogen. (Meanwhile, traditionalists can rest assured that the Bordelais classics—duck confit, foie gras, andouillette, frites cooked in duck fat—are still available, wonderful, and perfect to pair with the local tipple.)

The city of Bordeaux itself, only three hours by TGV from Paris, is brimming with youth (it has one of the largest universities in France) and looking better than ever: a recent wide-scale sandblasting has given its buildings a luster not seen here in centuries. The city-sponsored École du Vin offers what it calls "ambitious yet unpretentious courses for everyone." These range from two-hour tastings to three-day weekend tours. For a customized education, James Bonnardel, an elegant young oenologist and exporter, is your man: he can gain you access to obscure châteaux—or fly you in a helicopter to a secluded riverside to sample unique white wines paired with Arcachon oysters. ✚

GUIDE, PAGE 269.

Chef Thierry Marx of Château Cordeillan-Bages. Right: the grounds of Château Beychevelle winery. Opposite: the Place des Quinconces.

Fondée en 1925
Le Bistrot des Négociants

Île de Ré

BY THE BEAUTIFUL SEA

FRANCE IS RICH in coastline, but not so rich in islands. Which is fine with the French. What islands France has are not terribly famous, and are thus relatively untouristed, guaranteeing a local experience. Usually travelers have to do handstands for this kind of access, but visitors to Île de Ré are readily inducted into the highly codified French way of life on the sea.

Two miles off the coast, about two hours north of Bordeaux, Île de Ré is a 33-square-mile gem, with low-lying towns that are handsomely groomed, but not *too* groomed—hollyhocks push through the cobblestones. Locals are more engaging than anyone expects them to be. Only 18,000 people live here year-round, and though a toll bridge connects the island to the mainland, crowds have yet to overwhelm Ré. On even the busiest summer days you'll find a parking place. But bicycles are the preferred means of locomotion: 62 miles of paved bike paths wend across the island, passing oyster parks, potato fields, a bird reserve, and salt pans where *fleur de sel* is harvested.

And in recent years Ré's lodgings have greatly improved. Directly on the port in St.-Martin-de-Ré, the seven-room Le Corps de Garde occupies a 17th-century watchhouse. Organdy canopies frame quilt-covered beds, and views of the harbor and sea are swoon-inducing. The atmosphere is beachy, not buttoned-down, and beyond charming. Just like the island itself. ✚

GUIDE, PAGE 269.

The staff of Au Bord d'un Zinc show off the day's catch, right. Far right: Inside Le Corps de Garde's entryway. Below: On the harbor in St.-Martin-de-Ré. Opposite: Biking through Île de Ré.

T+L Tip

Don't miss the chance to try an order of vanet, a local shellfish recalling a scallop, but about 20 times smaller and 10 times as sweet. One great place for them is the classy new restaurant L'Avant Port.

Aveyron

EN ROUTE IN THE MIDI-PYRENEES

CLEARLY, IT IS A MISTAKE to arrive in a French provincial village on a Sunday, unless you are looking to understand why Madame Bovary felt she had to have some action or die. And there is no slower clock than that which ticks through the day of rest in the sparsely populated, largely unknown *département* of Aveyron, in the Midi-Pyrénées. Full of dairy farms and eccentric hamlets, Aveyron is *la France profonde,* the heartland that Parisians seldom visit and cannot fathom, but where there is some of the world's most stunning, diverse countryside, most of it unspoiled. Peaceful lakes are an hour's drive from vertiginous peaks; deep valleys edge eerie limestone plateaus; a thousand castles jog alongside Gallo-Roman ruins. Rodez, the region's hub, is the most dormant of towns. Its Musée Fenaille displays 5,000-year-old monoliths carved with stoic human faces.

Yet nearby, Norman Foster's 2004 Millau Viaduct, the world's tallest bridge and an unmatched feat of green engineering, offers a direct leap from prehistory to the 21st century. You can buy the famous knives of Laguiole at a Philippe Starck–designed factory, then dine on *gargouillou*—a melange of 50 roasted vegetables—at Michel Bras's Michelin three-starred Hôtel-Restaurant Bras.

Still, it is quiet in these parts. "Not everyone gets it," says local resident Bruno da Silva. "People come here and drive up to the plateau and come back and say to me, 'But there's nothing there.' How can I answer them? What is nothing for them is everything for us." ✚

GUIDE, PAGE 269.

The village of Najac and its 12th-century château. Opposite, from far left: The glass-walled dining room at Hôtel-Restaurant Bras; Véronique Bras, Michel Bras's daughter-in-law; the Millau Viaduct.

Brussels

WHAT'S OLD IS NEW AGAIN

POOR BRUSSELS. Its role as capital of the European Union and home base of NATO suggests a city of functionaries and bureaucrats: stolid, good for business (and breweries), hardly the center of cool. The reputation for stylishness belongs to Paris, of course—except among the cognoscenti, who know that Brussels, a 1,000-year-old city of a million-plus residents, is every bit as radical in fashion, and as adventuresome in cuisine—and much more fun to plunder for antiques.

The Place du Grand Sablon, a sweeping cobblestoned square, is the premier address for fine pieces. There's the small weekly antiques market: on Saturdays and Sundays, jaunty red-and-green-striped stalls offer brass candlesticks, handmade clocks and boxes, and wafer-thin porcelain dishes. The shops that radiate out from the square are equally tempting. Costermans, in business since 1839, is filled with 18th-century furniture, lanterns, and all manner of fireplace accessories—there's a courtyard of cast-iron firebacks that sit in rows like black stones in a forgotten graveyard. At Vincent Colet, you'll find remarkable 20th-century wares by Belgian designers with refreshingly unfamiliar names: Willy Van der Meeren, Marcel-Louis Baugniet. And Michel Lambrecht's shop draws American decorators for Korean ceramic lamps as well as for the owner's ingenious creations, such as light fixtures concocted from iron balustrade parts or pieces of an old wooden stool. "France has nicer objects from its rich past," Lambrecht says. "We Belgians never assume we are the best, so we must be much more inventive. ✚

GUIDE, PAGE 269.

Outside Vincent Colet, on Rue de la Régence. Opposite, from far left: Michel Lambrecht's Rue Watteau shop; Hans Bellmann-designed chairs at Vincent Colet.

Antwerp

A HISTORIC TOWN WITH A DIAMOND-CUTTING EDGE

Goose-liver terrine at Dôme Sur Mer, above left. Above center: Jewelry at Wouters & Hendrix. Above right: Dôme's marble-topped serving table. Opposite: Cathedral of Our Lady, near Market Square.

IT'S ONE OF EUROPE'S oldest and richest ports, but Antwerp has true 21st-century swagger, thanks largely to pioneering fashion designers Ann Demeulemeester and Dries Van Noten. Several other spots deemed to be the continent's "Next Hot Cities" have lately enjoyed their moments, and meanwhile Antwerpers have kept on doing what they do best: quietly creating absurdly stylish places to eat and shop.

South of the Old City, the Zurenborg and Zuid neighborhoods, for years described as up-and-coming, are now the glamour districts. Here you'll find fresh new restaurants—at white-tiled Fiskebar, you can sate cravings for ceviche and aquavit; Dôme sur Mer, an offshoot of Michelin-starred hot-ticket Dôme, is the perfect place for a split of Krug and a dozen Belon oysters.

The streets around the Nationalestraat brim with of-the-moment boutiques. There's the daring shoe store Elsa; the fuchsia-and-black treasure chest Baby Beluga, filled with frothy dresses; and Violetta & Vera Pepa, carrying the eponymous sisters' pared-down women's wear. (Upstairs you'll find Room National, the Pepas' petite B&B). Just east of the Nationalestraat area, art jeweler Wouters & Hendrix stands out and is definitely worth a visit—even here, in the diamond capital of the world. Exquisite pieces made of sterling silver or hand-hammered 18-karat gold are set with roughly tooled pearls and semiprecious stones.

And where is the city on the international fashion players' map? Just ask Yohji Yamamoto. He recently cut the ribbon on his Antwerp boutique—the largest Yamamoto store in the world. ✚

GUIDE, PAGE 269.

Ilulissat

FROZEN BEAUTY ABOVE THE ARCTIC CIRCLE

GREENLAND'S VAST EXPANSE of ice—up to two miles thick in places, and the size of continental Western Europe—has become a front line in the battle against global warming. Adventure travelers on a flight to the country sit shoulder to shoulder with scientists, politicians, and journalists.

Many tourists head first to Ilulissat ("Icebergs" in Inuit), on the west coast, just north of the Ilulissat Icefjord. The town's population of 6,000 makes it a megalopolis in Greenland. Here, civilization at its most cultured survives amid brutal wilderness. A tidy enclave of brightly painted houses sits on barren outcroppings of rock. Down the street from Pisiffik, a department store selling the latest duds from Denmark, two sinewy hunters hack a seal carcass into pieces.

Ilulissat's heart is its harbor, and for centuries fishing has been its lifeblood. The cold waters have spawned a fertile harvest of halibut, seal, and whale; now they lure visitors too. Tour boats navigate the massive bergs looming outside the harbor and carry passengers up to calving glaciers; mini-tsunamis surge forward with each falling chunk. By recent measurements, Greenland is losing 200 billion tons of ice per year. In Ilulissat, tundra flowers bloom weeks earlier than usual. Standing on a ridge, gazing at the white wilderness, you wonder how human activity could touch—let alone alter—this kingdom of ice. ✚

GUIDE, PAGE 270.

The hamlet of Ilulissat, 125 miles north of the Arctic Circle. Opposite, from far left: Local fisherman Peter Siegstad; Hotel Arctic's aluminum igloos.

Gästgivaregården
Etabl. 1640

A room at Loka Brunn's Parkvillan House, left. Below: Ost Café. Opposite: The Grythyttan Inn.

Grythyttan

LIFE AMONG THE CLOUDBERRIES

ONCE A SECRET retreat of Scandinavians, the village of Grythyttan, three hours' drive from Stockholm, has become a world-class destination that caters perfectly to city folks' getaway whims: a rustic walk, a rare Aalto chair, a delicious lunch. Rent a car and decompress as you head past lakes and dramatic boulder ridges, skirting the 17th-century hamlet of Nora.

The 368-year-old Grythyttan Inn is the area's most charming hotel—and a pilgrimage site for gourmands. Simple sunlit rooms are decorated with eclectic antiques and floral wallpapers. The restaurant serves roasted deer tenderloin with a porcini-filled potato roll and black-truffle gravy. Most of the menu is locally sourced (like the Bredsjö Blå sheep's-milk cheese), and there's a 7,000-bottle cellar. Nine miles south, at Loka Brunn, a 1720 mineral-spring spa, accommodations range from farmhouse-chic to Gustavian extravagance. Try the restaurant at the Nordic House of Culinary Art—set in a futuristic lakeside barn—for homey classics like pan-fried herring with mashed potatoes.

For a Scandinavian design fix, visit the Formens Hus design museum, in Hällefors. Exhibits include Alvar Aalto's bentwood chairs, and two re-created Midcentury Modern apartments. Save time for a tour of Grythyttan Vin, a vineyard celebrated for its fruity alchemy. Essential souvenir? A bottle of cloudberry wine. ✚

GUIDE, PAGE 270.

Åland Archipelago

ISLAND TO ISLAND ON THE BALTIC SEA

THERE ARE SOME 6,500 ISLANDS in the passage where the Baltic Sea collides with the Gulf of Bothnia. Many of them are no bigger than a football field, and only 65 have been settled—red wooden houses and terra-cotta–colored granite outcrops give these a vibrant hue. Vacationers from Norway, Denmark, Sweden, and the Finnish mainland come to hike oak and elm forests, admire ancient churches, and explore the rocky thumbs of land jutting up from the area's chilly seas.

Visitors arrive by plane or ferry at the linden-lined port in Mariehamn, the capital of the region and the biggest town on Åland, the main island, where most of the locals live. Other inhabited isles—Vardö, Brändö, Föglö—are joined by ferries and causeways. To the southeast is Kökar, a windswept moonscape with a graveyard said to hold the remains of Nordic pirates.

About 3,000 years ago, Åland was a teeming Viking outpost. Later, it belonged to Russia, and then Sweden, before being transferred to Finland in 1920. Swedish is still widely spoken, and Ålanders fly their own flag. The area is a bridge between nations, and its culture retains a staunch, Viking-like pride, interacting with, yet fiercely independent of, the world around it. ✚

GUIDE, PAGE 270.

Hotell Brudhäll, on a bay in Kökar. Opposite, from far left: The museum ship Pommern, in Mariehamn's western harbor; Kökar's 18th-century church; inside Indigo Restaurant & Bar.

Rotterdam

DUTCH BY DESIGN

HOLLAND'S SECOND CITY is smaller and edgier than Amsterdam (an hour north by train), and its thriving architecture and design scenes have earned Rotterdam a growing share of the spotlight. In typical Dutch fashion, the avant-garde here is leavened with a playful wit. Take, for instance, Piet Blom's dynamic Cube Houses, which resemble huge yellow dice in mid-toss, and have become a love-'em-or-hate-'em symbol of the city center. Downtown Rotterdam, destroyed by bombs in World War II, has largely been rebuilt in a daring modern style, and its ever-expanding skyline is a veritable survey of Dutch architects: there's Ben van Berkel's elegant Erasmus Bridge, native son Rem Koolhaas' Kunsthal museum, and the glass-and-steel apparition of the Netherlands Architecture Institute, designed by Jo Coenen.

The compact city is easily explored on foot or bike, or—better yet—by water taxi along the Nieuwe Maas river and several small harbors and canals. Rotterdam's port, the largest in Europe, has kept the city open to international influence, visible in the profusion of multiculti venues. At Las Palmas, the cascading crystal chandeliers in the hangar-sized dining room are a dramatic backdrop for the outstanding *fruits de mer* platter. At Hotel Bazar, each floor is designed to pay homage to a different part of the globe, with details like oversized Tigrinya script on the wall of an Eritrean-themed room. The café downstairs prepares excellent African and Middle Eastern food. For stirring city views, ride the high-speed elevator to the restaurant atop the 607-foot-high Euromast and take it all in with a glass of champagne. ✚

GUIDE, PAGE 270.

A view of the Euromast tower from the banks of the Nieuwe Maas river, above left. Above center: A Rotterdam local. Above right: Hotel Bazar's Eritrean-themed room. Opposite: Piet Blom's Cube Houses.

lin

CITY'S DYNAMIC CENTER

MITTE IS GERMAN for *middle*—an appropriate name for the most centrally located of Berlin's districts, which has been equally central to the city's identity though hundreds of years of political, social, and cultural seismic shifts. Post-unification, Mitte has become the vibrant heart of an energized metropolis that's still re-inventing itself, even as it struggles to honor its complex past. The streets around Unter den Linden, once a gray-on-gray grid of staid Prussian buildings housing the Communist bureaucracy, is now Berlin's smartest area, teeming with outposts of global luxury brands and host to Berlin's two chicest hotels: the

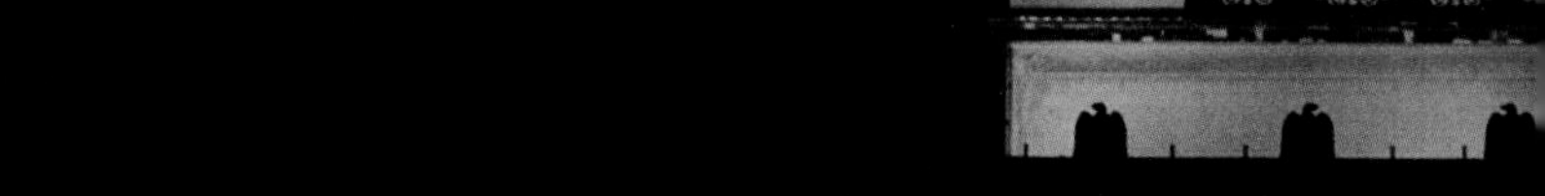

patrician Adlon Kempinski and Rocco Forte's swank Hotel de Rome, housed in the venerable old Dresdener Bank building. A few blocks south, the Spree River splits around the Museumsinsel, or Museum Island, a literal monument to Berlin's post-war resilience. After seeing their collections divided acrimoniously between East and West, the island's institutions now regularly host thoughtfully curated shows.

A different Mitte has evolved amid the winding cobbled lanes of Scheunenviertel, a sliver of a neighborhood that for centuries was home to Eastern European Jews fleeing persecution. The area's haphazard layout, heavily damaged during World War II, has been almost perfectly restored. Stroll through the charming Hackesche Höfe, a series of courtyards in the Secessionist style, then meander to Bonbonmacherei, where candy is made with ancient machines in a contemporary, minimalist space. Far from being incongruous, the contrast throws the colorful baroque confections into pleasing relief—as apt a metaphor for the new spirit of Berlin as you're bound to find. ✚

GUIDE, PAGE 270

An art in
tion in fr
of the A
Museum
Museum
in Berlin

St. Moritz

CHANGE COMES TO EUROPE'S WINTER RETREAT

The terrace at restaurant El Paradiso, overlooking the Engadine valley, below. Left: The pools at the Suvretta House hotel. Opposite: Instructor Olivier Molly skate-skis near the Silvaplana Castle.

THE ATMOSPHERE IN this spectacular Swiss aerie is different, thin and vodka-clear, as if imported from another dimension. The raw and menacing peaks—10,000 feet tall—loom over you like something out of an IMAX movie, close enough to touch. It's enough to make you feel giddy, and as you point your skis downhill don't be surprised if you're overcome by a sense of urgency—let's get going!

The unparalleled snow and pristine slopes gave this town a reputation as an adrenalin capital during the last century, and that hasn't changed. But St. Moritz, which used to be synonymous with old-school decorum and wealth, is suddenly re-energized and awash in new money—bewildering amounts of it. Villas and condos are springing up all over. The Shah of Iran's villa (built in the 1960's) just sold for about $34 million, and recent marquee developments include two from architect Norman Foster: Chesa Futura, a beautiful blob-like wooden apartment building, and Murezzan, his residential complex in the center of town. The cashmere and jewelry boutiques lining the streets are filled with >>

St. Moritz at dusk, above. Opposite, clockwise from top left: The terrace at El Paradiso; Reto Lamm, snowboard champion and entrepreneur, at Corviglia station; window seats in the lobby of Badrutt's Palace Hotel; general manager Hans Wiedemann (standing) and owner Hansjürg Badrutt, in the hotel's dining room.

fur-clad visitors—droves of them just in from Russia—who have never ridden a chairlift. One insider characterizes the phenomenon as "the Monte Carlo-ization of St. Moritz."

The main draw remains the skiing, a long day of which of course makes you hungry. Luckily, there are great places for lunch. Sit outside on a sheepskin-covered chair at El Paradiso and order their *Älpler Magronen*, a Swiss specialty of pasta with a beef *ragù*, topped with applesauce. Or stop at La Marmite, a local institution more than halfway up the mountain, in the funicular station at Corviglia. The menu focuses on venison, truffles, gravlax, and the like, and the food is remarkable—light and fresh, a relief after days of fondue and pasta.

Après-ski, stroll down the black and white marble corridor in the lobby of the Badrutt's Palace Hotel, and sink into one of the cavernous armchairs that overlook frozen, snow-covered Lake St. Moritz and an epic panorama of mountains. The property is still, as always, the sizzling center of the town's social scene, a fantastical combination of refined taste and winking sinfulness. ✚

GUIDE, PAGE 270.

Pio Cesare's Azienda Agricola vineyard, in Piedmont.

The Langhe

UNCORKING ITALY'S MOST EXCITING WINES

FOR CENTURIES, the undulating, vine-covered hills of the Langhe, a strip in the southern Piedmont region, existed as a place out of time. Nobody came, almost nobody left. But these days, acclaim for some of the new local bottlings—made from the nebbiolo grape, which itself is named for the area's trademark morning fog—is attracting wine pilgrims from all over. >>

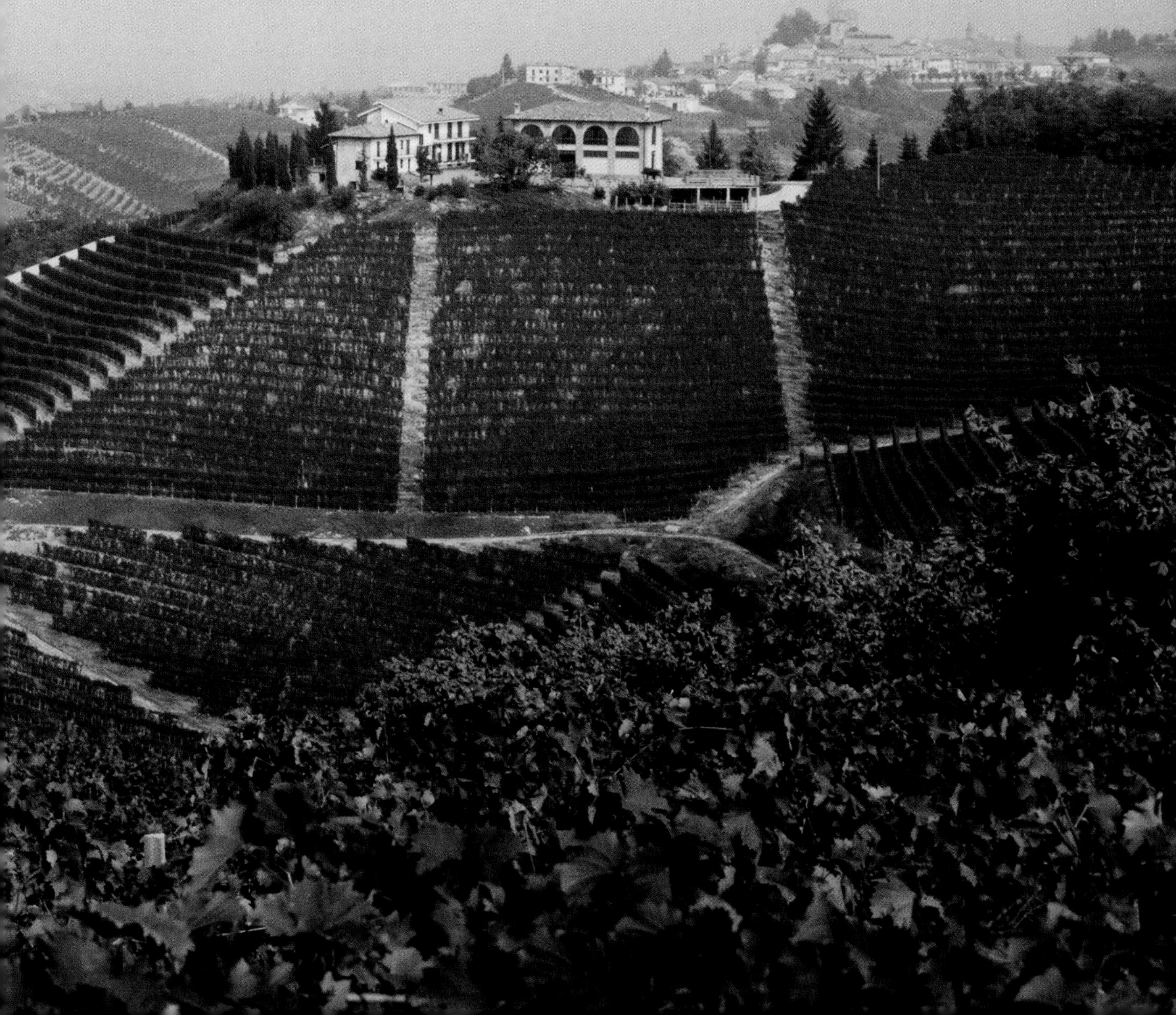

The pool at Villa Tiboldi, in Piedmont. Opposite, clockwise from far left: The sommelier at restaurant La Ciau del Tornavento; the restaurant's traditional agnolotti pasta; winemaker Giorgio Rivetti; the cellar at Pio Cesare.

Centuries-old villas have been converted into hotels, and the dining scene, which now includes a number of Michelin-starred establishments, is thriving.

A growing sophistication in local wine production is responsible for the area's rising fame. Many Langhe winemakers—led by Giorgio Rivetti of La Spinetta—are creating wines that are smoother and more potent than the old Barolos and Barbarescos, snipping nascent grapes from the vines in June to give those that remain a better chance to develop character and power. Modern technology is being used to understand why some vines yield better fruit than others. These newer wines beautifully express the terroir—and they don't need a decade of cellar time before they can be enjoyed.

In contrast, the wineries of Pio Cesare and several of his confrères, situated on some of the best vineyard sites in Barolo and Barbaresco, continue to produce traditional Piedmontese wines. These are rougher on the palate, requiring more time to savor and understand, but they give the sipper a taste of something that has been crafted like an heirloom. Says Cesare, "A real Barolo, it requires time to understand it, but when you do, you can't live without. It conquers you, sip by sip."

For the dedicated oenophile, these two philosophies of Langhe production make the experience of savoring the region's wines all the richer. They are the older and younger sons of Piedmontese wine culture, the heir and the innovator. One preserves a glorious past, while the other seeks its fortune in the future. ✚

GUIDE, PAGE 271.

T+L Tip
Most area wineries don't have scheduled tours. Try a few wines before leaving home, pick your favorites, then call ahead to request an appointment. You'll have an unforgettable time.

Emilia-Romagna

YOUR OWN PRIVATE RENAISSANCE

TOURS OF THE LAST SUPPER, in Milan, are booked months in advance. In Florence, admirers of Michelangelo's *David* stand cheek-by-jowl. Rome's Sistine Chapel beckons at the end of an insufferable line. What's an art pilgrim to do? Go to Emilia-Romagna. In the north-central region commonly associated with cattle farms and cheese, Roman, Byzantine, medieval, and Renaissance masters produced eye-popping art, and it's blessedly crowd-free.

Your base is Bologna, the province's capital, home to the oldest university in Europe—and sublime tortellini. (The city is the *caput mundi* of stuffed pasta.) Bologna's ornate basilicas and medieval churches contain some of Italy's most innovative, influential early sculpture. At the 13th-century Basilica of San Domenico lies the

tomb of Saint Dominic, upon which Nicola Pisano carved a short movie in marble, chronicling the life of the Dominican order's founder. Another master added his own touch: beside the sarcophogus kneels an angel carved by a young Michelango. The angel's face is a forerunner to his famous Delphic Sibyl in the Sistine Chapel, just as his figure of Saint Procolo, on the back of the tomb, is a *David* in the making.

A 40-minute scenic drive north is the pearl of Ferrara, a half-medieval, half-Renaissance architectural wonder. Sensitive planning and careful preservation of this dual character earned Ferrara the title of Italy's first "modern city." Stroll past elegant 16th-century houses along Corso Ercole I to reach the lavish Palazzo dei Diamanti, designed by visionary architect Biagio Rosetti; adorned with 12,000 rhomboid marble blocks, the palazzo seems constructed of gargantuan white diamonds.

Alternatively, drive an hour southeast to Ravenna, for the Basilica of San Vitale's sixth-century mosaics: showers of sparkling white angels and green and blue birds. Due south, in seaside Rimini, is Tempio Malatestiano, a Gothic cathedral inside a re-created Roman temple. This weird, ingenious, soaring concoction was the first true Renaissance exterior. And you can take it in at your own pace, without jostling for the perfect view. ✚

GUIDE, PAGE 271.

Ferrara's 12th-century duomo, above. Above left: The Piazza Maggiore in Bologna. Opposite, from far left: Mosaics in Ravenna's Galla Placidia; a first-century B.C. triumphal arch in Rimini; a Ferrara promenade.

The terrace at Ristorante Il Tramonto, high above Il Forno's port, left. Below: Aboard the water taxi to Frontone beach. Opposite: Bathers at Frontone.

Ponza

WHERE ROMANS HOLIDAY

WITH ITS HIGH white cliffs and craggy brown rocks, the island of Ponza, off Italy's western coast, appears as a shocking interruption in the serene Tyrrhenian Sea. A penal colony in the days of the Roman Empire, this remote volcanic atoll looks from a distance impossible to scale. Get a little closer and you see tidy vineyards, modest villas painted in appealing colors, and intimate coves sheltering small, rocky beaches.

Yes, this four-square-mile bump has been rediscovered—by today's Romans and Neapolitans, who escape here on summer weekends and have somehow managed to keep Ponza to themselves. Developers have yet to penetrate; there is only a smattering of small hotels and rental villas. The activities menu is blissfully basic: swimming and snorkeling, lingering in trattorias over impossibly fresh seafood, and gazing at the sea. A single bus loops the main road between Ponza, the main port, and Le Forna, near the island's northern tip. The best beaches are inaccessible by land, unless you're in the mood to rappel—instead, hop a water taxi to Frontone (a family-friendly spot with chairs and sun umbrellas for rent) or, better yet, hire a boat to explore the island's myriad hidden coves. ✚

GUIDE, PAGE 271.

Via Corrado Nicolaci, in Noto, left. Below: Suckling-pig pork chop at Ragusa's Ristorante Duomo. Opposite: The owners (seated) and chef of Caol Ishka, in the hotel's dining room.

Sicily

A FRONTIER OF ITALIAN COOKING

THE BOTTOM OF SICILY lies farther south than the top of Tunisia, so it's no surprise that the landscape here—rugged limestone gorges, carob plantations, and quiet farms—is neither European nor African, but something intriguingly in-between. Historically, Italians and other Europeans have retreated to this part of the island for peace and classic comfort food like *spaghetti alla Norma* (pasta with eggplant and ricotta in tomato sauce). But in recent years, foodies have been beating a path to the area's Baroque towns, where daring local chefs have begun to tweak time-honored recipes.

Take your first bite in the ancient Ionian Coast city of Siracusa, where the Anapo River flows out of the mountains. Beside the river is Caol Ishka, a boutique hotel with 10 rustic-chic rooms distributed among 19th-century stone farm buildings. At the hotel's Zafferano Bistrot, chef Massimo Giaquinta pairs traditional ingredients (sautéed prawns that have been marinated in lemon and anchovies) >>

Siracusa's 17th-century Piazza del Duomo, left. Opposite, clockwise from top left: Poolside at Caol Ishka; the wine-tasting room at COS; gnocchi with Gorgonzola sauce and cherry-tomato coulis, at Caol Ishka's restaurant; preparing pastry envelopes at Antica Dolceria Bonajuto.

with new (grouper roe and soft ricotta). A 40-minute drive south takes you to the highland town of Noto, where Salvatore Guarino serves epic lunches at the Masseria degli Ulivi. One tempting course: *filetto* of meltingly tender beef on a bed of risotto laced with verbena. For dessert, move on to Caffè Sicilia, the laboratory of culinary alchemist Corrado Assenza, for a zabaglione with 800 years of Sicilian history in each mouthful: extravagant swirls of cream and sugar from the Spanish, almond flour and honey from the Arabs. Inland, in Modica, you'll find one of the strongest and most unyielding tastes in Sicily: that of cold-processed chocolate from the Antica Dolceria Bonajuto, used to flavor the shop's famous pastry envelopes stuffed with eggplant or meat. The family-run firm, now in the hands of a new generation, has also tapped into the vogue for salty sweets.

No food-focused swing through southeastern Sicily is complete without a visit to the standard-bearer of the island's culinary revolution: the elegant Ristorante Duomo, in Ragusa. Here, chef Ciccio Sultano has gained fame—and two Michelin stars—for his impeccably sourced ingredients and inventive take on classic Sicilian cooking. Dig into lamb chops braised in jasmine honey and crusted with pistachios and you'll understand why this is where the region's chefs themselves come to eat—and to look for inspiration. ✚

GUIDE, PAGE 271.

A terrace at Hotel Margarita. Opposite, top left: Kaladi Beach. Opposite, bottom left: Looking out at the Ionian Sea.

Kíthira

THE INSIDER'S GREEK ISLAND

THE CARDINAL RULE for avoiding Greece's many tourist traps—never eat at a restaurant named Zorba's—can be blithely ignored on Kíthira. This Ionian isle has the blindingly white houses and broad beaches found in the Cyclades, but instead of being bare and volcanic, Kíthira is lush and green. Best of all, locals and summer residents have conspired to keep its caves, coves, and azure bays a secret—yet it's just a 45-minute nonstop flight from Athens.

Hora, the hilltop capital, is an ideal base, with friendly cafés for sipping iced coffee and lolling. Stay at Hotel Margarita, a 12-room mansion converted by Parisian expats. A mile to the east lies crescent-shaped Kapsali beach, ringed by tavernas and retro-chic blue-and-white changing booths.

The island's thirty miles of coastline, flowering mountains, and Byzantine villages offer fantastic day trips. Visit the Agia Sophia cave, with stalagmites, stalactites, and walls painted with icons by 19th-century sailors; picture-perfect Mylopotamos, its square filled with backgammon players; the torrential Neraides waterfall; and the sparkling waters off Kaladi Beach. When you return to Hora, dine at Zorba's—a rooftop restaurant where the food (impeccable souvlaki, juicy tomato salad) and service (the gregarious owner) are decidedly authentic and utterly satisfying. ✚

GUIDE, PAGE 271.

EASTERN EUROPE

Tending cows along a riverbank in Romania's Danube Delta.

Hotel Nové Lázně's Roman bath. Opposite, clockwise from top left: The Imperial Cabin at Hotel Nové Lázně ; a rig for hire in Marienbad's Kurpark; a spring fountain in Karlsbad.

Marienbad

STEEPED IN THE WATERS OF HISTORY

YOU REACH MARIENBAD as you would an enchanted castle: through a dense, dark wood on a road that winds back so often, you're sure you must be lost. Emerging onto the streets of the small Czech town, you *know* this is a fairy tale. Hapsburg-era hotels look like pastel desserts iced with sugar roses. Ornate 19th-century spas teem with caryatids, Tritons, nymphs, and other magical creatures.

The spa triangle of Marienbad, Karlsbad, and Franzensbad sits on a plateau near the Ore Mountains, two hours' drive from Prague. Grandees of the empire took the cure here—as did Frédéric Chopin, Johann Strauss, and Mark Twain. The springs flow from elaborate grottoes, and guests still spend less time soaking in the waters than imbibing them.

On the town's older streets, nearly all visitors clutch a ceramic cup, ready to catch the liquids— icy, scalding, tasteless, sulfurous, fizzy, flat—that pour from every fountain, each of which promises a remedy for some ailment. Broaden your idea of what a spa should be: instead of a facial, try a carbon bath; skip yoga for "inhalation exercises." Explore a lost way of life at the 112-year-old Hotel Nové Lázně, where you can even visit Edward VII's gilded Royal Cabin bath. ✚

GUIDE, PAGE 273.

The mausoleum of Petar II Petrovic Njegoš, a 19th-century prince-bishop of Montenegro, atop Mount Lovćen.

Montenegro

SCALING THE HEIGHTS IN THE BALKANS

THE FEELING ONE GETS when crossing the border into Montenegro is that this is the last wild place in Europe. Lack of development has helped keep Montenegro's natural beauty mostly untouched, its tradition of friendliness toward visitors uncorrupted, and the culture of its ancient civilization intact. At the southern end of the former Yugoslavia, this compact and newly sovereign state (it became independent from Serbia in 2006) makes for a thrill-a-minute, two- to three-day drive. It's certainly not hard to reach: Do as many visitors do and fly into neighboring Croatia; turn left out of the Dubrovnik airport and a half hour later you're at the border. >>

A mountain village in Durmitor National Park, left. Opposite, clockwise from top left: Inside the royal palace in Cetinje; Morača Monastery, near Kolašin; selling wild berries in Durmitor; overlooking the Bay of Kotor from Perast.

T+L Tip
During the summer, it's possible to climb the snow-capped peaks of the Dinaric Alps and swim in the sparkling blue waters of the Adriatic in the same day.

Just over 35 miles east lies the UNESCO-protected town of Perast, a museum piece of balconied waterfront mansions and quiet backstreets overgrown with fig trees and oleander. In the walled city of Kotor, marble-flagged squares and medieval buildings recall the once untrammeled Dubrovnik. Follow the "Old Road"—a series of hairpin bends tracing a zigzag mule track—into the mountains, and be rewarded with dazzling views of the Bay of Kotor far below, looking like a spill of quicksilver.

From here the road snakes through tiny hamlets to Cetinje, Montenegro's former royal capital, set in a green bowl among rocky outcroppings. Outside the city rise the twin peaks of Lovćen, a mountain held sacred by Montenegrins; poised on a nearby ridge like a hunched stone eagle is the mausoleum of Prince-Bishop Petar II Petrović, who died in 1851 at the age of 38 and is venerated as the wise and saintly father of his country. Atop a windswept platform nearby, the whole nation is visible, from the shining Adriatic to the snow-tipped Durmitor range, approximately 130 miles north.

With its wildflower-covered meadows and glistening glacial lakes (called "mountain eyes"), Durmitor National Park reveals an entirely different side of the country, and is well worth the four-hour drive inland from the coast. Stop for wild berries and honey at roadside stands en route. Circling back to Cetinje, don't miss the 13th-century Morača Monastery, near the town of Kolašin. Like many Orthodox abbeys here, Morača has some impressive medieval and Baroque frescoes, but it's most alluring for being a very active place of worship. Despite increasing numbers of visitors, the tidy enclave, with its orchards, beehives, and rose-draped cloisters, still offers a profound sense of continuity and peace. ✚

GUIDE, PAGE 273.

Sarajevo

FROM THE ASHES OF WAR, A SURPRISING REBIRTH

On warm spring days, when the fog finally lifts from the surrounding hills, scarcely a table is to be had at the long line of cafés stretching from the cathedral in Centar, Sarajevo's old imperial quarter. Friends arrive in twos or threes, then gather fresh company; this is a small town, and nobody's a stranger. Young women strut by—and circle back, in case they weren't noticed.

In 1992, when Yugoslavia collapsed into war, the Serbian troops set up positions in the mist-shrouded hills and laid siege to the city for almost four years. Since the coming of peace, Sarajevo has been repairing the damage at a rapid rate, restoring its singularly graceful melding of Islamic and Western life and culture. Swoop-neck coffeepots, hammered copper trays, carpet stalls in the bazaar, and the echoing calls of the muezzin remind one of Cairo or Fez. Yet this is still Europe, and so the Spanish-tiled roofs have overhanging eaves and the alleys do not meander, but intersect at right angles.

Memories of the war live on, part of the land's recovery. In tranquil Mostar, about two hours' drive southwest of Sarajevo, a glorious white stone bridge arcs high above the shining Neretva River. The bridge, destroyed in the fighting, has been reconstructed using the same local stone and original medieval engineering. It's breathtaking: a true emblem of an irreplaceable region's near death, and resurrection. ✚

GUIDE, PAGE 273.

A Muslim woman in Sarajevo's Turkish Quarter, above. Above left: A rug shop on Saraci Street. Opposite: The bridge at Mostar, reconstructed after the war.

Danube Delta

ONE OF EUROPE'S LAST FRONTIERS

THESE WILDLIFE-RICH WETLANDS in Romania, 180 miles northeast of Bucharest, frame one of the most beautiful stretches of Europe's second-longest river. Here, the Danube's banks attract millions of birds migrating from the rest of Europe, Africa, and the Middle East. In the spring, pelicans touch down in 1,000-strong flights. The waters hold at least 80 fish species, including pike, sander, and yard-long sevruga sturgeon that yield top-grade caviar. Venture into the surrounding countryside, and you find

a land of medieval hamlets, monasteries, wineries, and garden-fringed farmers' cottages.

Until the 2005 arrival of the Delta Nature Resort, Romania's first new high-end property in decades, travel to this area was the sole province of the backpack brigade. Today, outdoors enthusiasts, sport fishermen, and wealthy Romanians convene at the low-impact, 32-acre enclave of villas, where the flourishes—hand-loomed carpets, dark wood furniture—are intentionally subtle.

But the real draw is the land itself—and the opportunities the resort provides for exploring it. You can cruise the river to witness cormorant colonies nesting in the willows and wild poplars, sample Merlots and Cabernet Sauvignons at the 400-year-old Sarica Niculitzel winery, and lunch on quail eggs and roast duck in the refectory of the 1846 Saon Monastery.

And, of course, get your daily dose of caviar. ✚

GUIDE, PAGE 273.

The small chapel at the Saon Monastery, above. Opposite, from far left: The Angler's Bar at the Delta Nature Resort; a horse-drawn carriage on a lane near the resort.

Kiev

UKRAINE'S CAPITAL COMES OF AGE

REMINDERS OF THE PAST—golden onion domes, hammer-and-sickle insignia—are everywhere in Kiev. Yet, since late 2004, when a mass street protest ushered in the Orange Revolution, Ukraine's capital has undergone furious changes. Western investment has brought new hotels, high-end shops, and restaurants galore. And now that the state has dropped visa requirements for Western travelers, Kiev stands one EasyJet route away from becoming another perfectly polished

tourist site. Fortunately, there is still time to taste this town's heady cocktail of before and after.

Base yourself on the cosmopolitan right bank of the Dnieper River, with its humming public squares, beer gardens, and folk dancers performing in front of ancient cathedrals. The Radisson SAS Hotel, a 1903 gem, is just blocks from Maydan Nezalezhnosti (Independence Square), the heart of the city, where great government and mercantile buildings ring a plaza that contains a 5,000-jet fountain called the Friendship of Nations. The Hyatt Regency, near St. Michael's Square, has views of gilded St. Sophia Cathedral and St. Michael's monastery, both completed in the 1050's.

The neighborhood's markets are as beloved as the plazas. On Andreevsky Spusk, browsers can find one-off souvenirs—a lacquered jewelry box, czarist-era rubles—among the nesting dolls and fake Soviet-insignia pins. At Bessarabsky Market, in a 1912 rotunda, women in flowered head scarves sell caviar, fruit, flowers, and honey.

For 21st-century browsing, try the Passazh complex on Khreshchatyk, showing Russian and Ukrainian fashion designers. For contemporary European art—Western and Eastern—there's the astonishingly mod Pinchuk Art Centre, brainchild of Victor Pinchuk, oligarch and son-in-law of ex-president Leonid Kuchma.

Restaurants are branching out from blinis and borscht: Belvedere specializes in Pan-Asian fare; Ikra is known for its seafood. The after-hours spot is Decadence House, an Art Deco room lit by candles and sugarplum-shaped chandeliers. Babuin, a bookstore-bar-cabaret club, is the place to decompress after a few dizzying days in this fast-evolving town. ✚

GUIDE, PAGE 273.

The café in the Pinchuk Art Centre, above. Above left: St. Michael's gold-domed monastery. Opposite: Locals in traditional folk dress, overlooking the Dnieper River.

Moscow

WELCOME TO THE NEW, NEW RUSSIA

St. Basil's Cathedral, crowning Red Square. Opposite, clockwise from left: Art 4 owner Igor Markin with gallerist Motya Petrakova; the Ritz-Carlton's glassed-in roof bar; a cozy corner in Art 4.

LOUD MONEY and brutish excess defined 1990's Moscow, but today a more sophisticated story is unfolding. Hip galleries, restaurants, and fashion boutiques (for those famously dressed-to-kill Muscovites) are springing up everywhere in the old Communist cityscape. And the outlandish club scene—where you'll still see crude-oil barons stumbling past bouncers at 6 a.m.—has become more democratic, even as the Kremlin veers in the opposite direction. In short, a new kind of Russian culture is being born. "It's a great time to start anything," says one entrepreneur. "We have lost our history. But because of this we're fresh, young, and a little bit wild."

Take the most exciting museum to open in Moscow in the past century: Art 4, which gleefully displays totalitarian-stamped vistas by seventies Pop artist Erik Bulatov, cocktails of violence and buffoonery by eighties painter Konstantin Zvezdochetov, and a provocative (for Russia, anyway) photograph of two militiamen kissing. The New Tretyakov Gallery houses Moscow's must-see collection of early-20th-century art by Malevich, Goncharova, and Chagall, among others. And megaboutique Tsum, a worthy stop on the worldwide shopping circuit, still attracts slim-thighed trophy wives with its $1,000 dresses in sizes two and four.

The Tsum set dines in the over-the-top Czarist room at aptly named the Most, where king crab fresh from Vladivostok is served broiled with spinach and Parmesan, and roast Barbary duck is carved tableside. Open round the clock, Café Pushkin is another contender for the title of Moscow's ultimate fine-Russian-cuisine restaurant. Sleep it off at the Ritz-Carlton Moscow, a 2007 debutant and the best new hotel in town, with all the veined marble, velvet silks, and crisp linens you could ask for—plus knockout Kremlin views from its upper (dare we say haute?) floors. ✚

GUIDE, PAGE 273.

T+L Tip

A visa is still required for entry into Russia. All visa applicants must have a tourist invitation; many hotels will supply one for a small fee. For more information, go to waytorussia.net or expresstorussia.com.

Istanbul

A ONCE-BELOVED NEIGHBORHOOD, BACK ON THE MAP

AT THE TURN of the 20th century, Turks dressed to the nines to promenade along the Parisian-style arcades of Beyoğlu, the age-old cosmopolitan heart of Istanbul, just across the Golden Horn inlet from Sultanahmet, the city's historic center. After a period of neglect in the 1980's, the district is reclaiming its name as Istanbul's favorite playground. And although Starbuck-ization is taking its toll on the famed main artery, Istiklal Caddesi, the backstreets are an enticing tangle of kebab dives, hipster clubs, grungy boutiques, and lounges with glamorous Bosporus views. Don't miss Alaturca, a shop housed in a 19th-century mansion and crammed with exquisite antique tableware, embroideries, and kilims, or confectioner Haci Bekir, where the *lokum,* or Turkish delight, is flavored with mint and roses.

Take as home base the stylish property Ansen Suites—10 crisp, airy rooms, some with windows onto the Golden Horn—or Misafir Suites, a tiny inn featuring Designer Guild textiles and marble bathrooms fit for a pasha.

Follow your nose to get your bearings: the scented soul of old Beyoğlu is in its *meyhane,* or traditional drinking houses, such as Refik and Yakup 2, where locals sip raki, a powerful anise liqueur, and nosh on spicy meatballs and stuffed peppers. For a dose of the new sophistication, sample the au courant fare (smoked lamb with walnut *pistou;* lavender-and-honey-glazed chicken), panoramic city views, and Scandinavian-inspired design at Mikla. Then hit Babylon, the edgy live-music venue that sparked the area's renaissance. Make your grand finale Nu Pera, a bar-and-restaurant complex that's Beyoğlu's party central. The rooftop lounge is mobbed by smartly clad Istanbul scene-makers, once again getting their groove on. ✚

GUIDE, PAGE 273.

Confections at Haci Bekir, below. Center: The dining room at Mikla. Right: Antique housewares at Alaturca. Opposite: Istiklal Caddesi, Beyoğlu's main drag.

MHP
ROBERT'S COFFEE
TAKSI
34 TBJ 28
ÖNDER OTO

A cityscape of Tunis, in Tunisia, as seen from the minaret of the Zitouna, or Great Mosque.

AFRICA + THE MIDDLE EAST

Addis Ababa

THE NEW BUZZ IN ETHIOPIA

THERE'S CHANGE IN THE AIR in Africa's second-most populous country. It's been building, slowly, since the end of the repressive Mengistu regime in 1991; exiles have returned, bringing investment money and new confidence. Their spirit now pervades Ethiopia's lofty capital, from its outskirts (overlooked by 10,000-foot Mount Entoto) to its hopping downtown nightclubs and cafés. Despite ongoing frustrations—tensions with Somalia, continued poverty, a government shackled by bureaucracy—Addis Ababa is bursting with creative energy, and even optimism.

If this city of 3.6 million has a heart, it's the *merkato,* Africa's largest open-air market, where miles of tin stalls are divided by narrow alleys into entire districts of spices, fresh produce, coffee, and herbed butter. No wonder the city's cuisine—savory purées and stews scooped up with *injera,* a spongy flatbread—is such a draw. Try it at Habesha, a patio restaurant beloved by star New York chef Marcus Samuelsson. Then hit barnlike Gonder Tej Bet for housemade *tej,* a deep-gold honey wine that suggests a turmeric-spiked Riesling. It tastes of magic: it tastes of Addis Ababa. ✚

GUIDE, PAGE 275.

A local woman at the *merkato.* Opposite, from far left: The Hilton Addis Ababa's pool; a traditional meal of fried Nile perch with *shiro* and *doro wet* at Habesha.

Madagascar

INTO THE WILD, GENTLY

THERE IS NOTHING dangerous or threatening in Madagascar. On mainland African safaris you have to stay in a vehicle, because lions will eat you and hippos will trample you and rhinos and buffalo will charge. In Madagascar, the animals only look at you with wide-eyed wonder. Whole swaths of the world's fourth-largest island (it's 980 miles long and 360 miles wide) remain only semi-explored. Called by some ecologists "the eighth continent"—because it broke off from Africa's eastern coast some 160 million years ago and developed in isolation—Madagascar rivals Brazil in its biodiversity. New species are found regularly, including some that were supposed extinct. The bizarre flora and fauna seem to be the result of a mad collaboration among Dr. Seuss, Jim Henson, and God; the green, green rice paddies, the red, red earth, and the blue, blue sea are like a child's drawing in crayon.

The French took over the island in the late 19th century and departed in 1958, leaving their language behind. Madagascar's capital city, Antananarivo, sits on a high plateau and is lovely in its own right. But you'll want to spend the bulk of your time in the wild—exploring the bevy of national parks; snorkeling along the pristine reefs >>

A baobab tree in Beza-Mahafaly. Opposite, from far left: The view from Nosy Komba; a baby chameleon (*Calumma nasuta*).

Locals at Jardin Vanille Beach, on Nosy Komba, above. Opposite, clockwise from top left: A guide in Nosy Komba's Ampangoriana village; one of the island's giant baobab trees; a black-and-white ruffed lemur; sahondra flowers at Vakôna Forest Lodge.

that ring outer islands such as Nosy Komba; and staying at the fabulously remote-feeling Vakôna Forest Lodge, tucked in a jungle grove. Roads in Madagascar are generally potholed and twisting, and best navigated with a hired car and driver—first-time visitors generally sign on with a tour company and get around by four-wheel-drive vehicle, boat, and plane.

Along the way you may come upon some of the island's more exotic inhabitants, such as the inch-long Brookesia minima chameleon, one of the smallest vertebrates on earth. But the highlight of your explorations will surely be the astonishing 39 varieties of lemurs, Madagascar's odd primates, who are shy and mild but not at all astonished by your presence, as if you belonged there. As far as they're concerned, you do: at the Beza-Mahafaly reserve, the lemurs have been observing scientists observing them for 30 years. Whole families of them dance right across the road and swing in plain sight through the baobab trees, but the animals can also convey a remarkable stillness and grace. Among the most peaceful sights you encounter might be that of a solitary lemur, bright eyes blinking in a black-and-white face, sitting silently in the golden, late-afternoon light, seeming to glow with its own private radiance. ✚

GUIDE, PAGE 275.

Madikwe Private Game Reserve

ZEBRAS, ELEPHANTS, AND RHINOS—UP CLOSE AND PERSONAL

THE MADIKWE PRIVATE Game Reserve, in the northwestern corner of South Africa, is two safaris in one: part Kalahari Desert, part bush country. The malaria-free 185,000-acre refuge is ideal for spotting giraffes as well as rare wild dogs and the furry tree-dwelling primates known as bush babies.

Set between the slopes of two rolling hills, rustic-chic Madikwe Safari Lodge, built of thatch and stone, has 20 suites filled with antique Bauer travel chests and baskets from the local Tswana tribes; some also have private plunge pools. For the most privacy, book a spot in the smaller, four-suite West Camp—where you can watch animals crossing the plains while you soak in a bronze-plated bath tub. More active naturalists can schedule a morning game drive in an open-top Jeep. If you're lucky, you'll come across elephants, rhinos, and lions, or even rarely seen cheetahs.

Back at the lodge, you can choose to join the group for an alfresco dinner around the camp's fire pit, or arrange to have a lantern-lit meal served on the deck of your suite. The Pan-African menu includes Afrikaner *potjie,* a traditional stew of game meat slowly braised in a cast-iron soup pot. Don't miss the *malva* pudding—sticky-toffee cake doused with butterscotch sauce.

On evening drives, guests are served glasses of iced *mampoer,* a fruit-based Afrikaner eau-de-vie, while they watch the sun setting behind the Marico River. Wherever you go, you won't see another person for miles—except, of course, for your smiling comrades. ✚

GUIDE, PAGE 275.

T+L Tip
Madikwe Safari Lodge's chef, Lavuis Tlhagwane, offers private cooking lessons upon request. Learn to make African tamales stuffed with local corn and a sweet potato filling.

A vista at Madikwe Private Game Reserve. Opposite: Madikwe Safari Lodge's dining room.

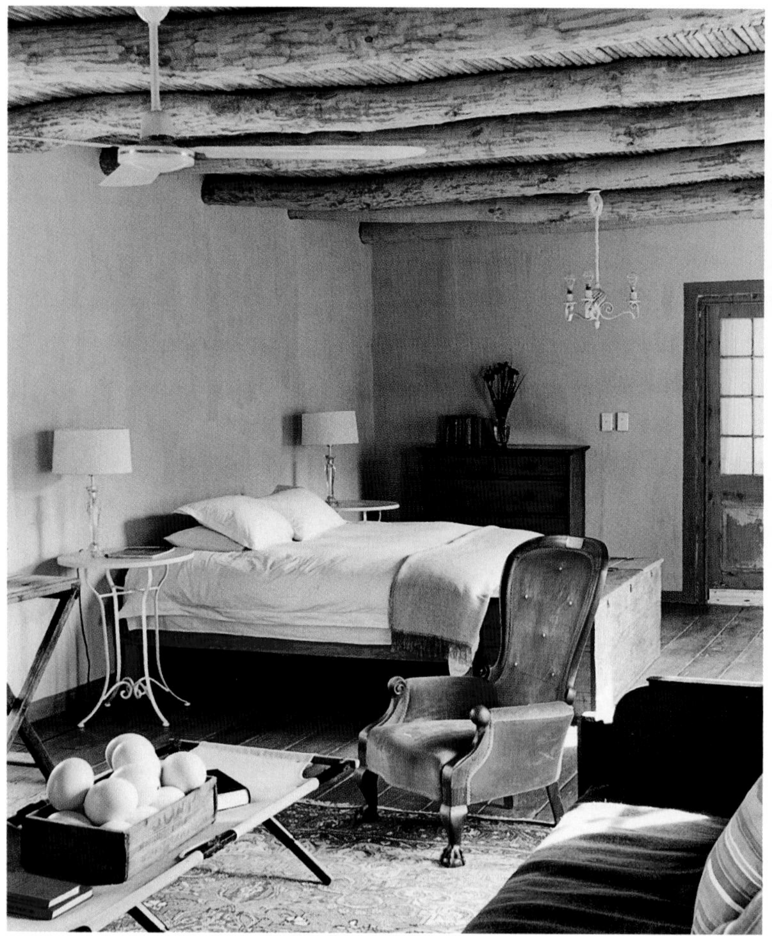

The Karoo

A DRIVE ACROSS THE CAPE PLAINS

SOUTH AFRICA'S VAST, semidesert Karoo region was once a veritable no-man's land. Now, the villages joined by its dusty roads have been given new life by creative ex-urbanites, making it well worth a long weekend's drive from Cape Town.

Begin in Barrydale, gateway to the Little Karoo, where Route 62 flattens out between sand and fynbos scrub and the sky takes on the earth's curve. Have lunch at Ronnies Sex Shop—a beloved roadside burger joint named to draw business. Go on to Calitzdorp, an enclave of Cape Dutch houses and vineyards producing rich fortified wines. Stop overnight in Oudtshoorn, at Boesmanskop, a tiny, charming inn set in jungly gardens, or at the Feather Palace guest ranch, once an ostrich farm.

In the morning, cross the majestic red-rock Swartberg Pass; from the summit, the Great Karoo seems to stretch forever. The road then descends gently to Prince Albert, a serene town of orchards and vines—try the sublime Shiraz Reserve at Bergwater Vineyards, and meaty Manzanilla olives at Swartrivier farm. Next, take the Montagu Pass over the verdant Outeniqua Mountains to the Garden Route, where rusty desert becomes evergreen forest, then glinting blue coast. On your way to Knysna, stop at Wilderness Beach and wash off the dust in wild cerulean waves. ✚

GUIDE, PAGE 275.

The Indian Ocean, near Knysna. Opposite, from far left: Upstairs at the two-room Boesmanskop inn; an ostrich farm along Route 62.

Swartland

A WINE REGION ON THE RISE

THE SWARTLAND—literally "black land," named for the color of its tangled undergrowth—extends north along South Africa's Atlantic coast from the outskirts of Cape Town. A beautiful region of mountains, gabled Cape Dutch architecture, and farmland, it's recently been drawing daytripping Cape Towners with a cluster of emerging vineyards.

After years of selling grapes—Shiraz, Cabernet, and some of the country's best Chenin Blanc—to top producers in Stellenbosch and Paarl, Swartland growers are finally making their own wines. In

Allesverloren Wine Estate's turreted 18th-century cottage, you can sample South Africa's most sought-after port, a seven-grape field blend. At idyllic Kloovenburg, perfectionist Pieter du Toit crafts only 16,000 six-bottle cases per year of his world-class Cabernet blends, including the much-sought-after Eight Feet (bottled by his four sons). Newcomer Pulpit Rock focuses on single-grape wines, including one of South Africa's most lauded Pinotages and a warm, earthy Shiraz—both ideal with sausage made from local game by owner Ernest Brink. The Sadie Family Estate—a shed with an old brick barrel room and no visitor amenities—sits on a rutted dirt road behind Paardeburg Mountain. Here, proprietor Eben Sadie, back from a tour of the world's top wineries, offers his incomparable Syrah-based Columella—and as much info on Swartland terroir as you'd truly like to know. ✚

GUIDE, PAGE 275.

The veranda at Swartland's Royal Hotel, above. Left: Looking across the Riebeek Valley. Far left: Winemaker Eben Sadie at the Sadie Family Estate.

Tunis

AN ENCHANTED, CENTURIES-OLD CITY

A dining room at Dar el Jeld, a restaurant set in a medina palace, above. Above left: A Roman mosaic at the Bardo National Museum. Opposite: The minaret of the Zitouna, or Great Mosque.

FOR MANY VISITORS, Tunis is a jumping-off point, the city en route to the Mediterranean resorts clustered on its northern coast. Yet Tunisia's capital offers plenty of reasons to linger.

The seventh-century medina is abuzz with activity, a labyrinth of cobblestoned streets, columned archways, and whitewashed houses. Rising above it is the extraordinary Zitouna, or Great Mosque. Even though it's off-limits to non-Muslims, it's worth a stop just for the chance to glimpse into its main prayer hall, filled with kilims and massive chandeliers.

Several of the medina's ancient structures have been transformed specifically to welcome guests. Salah Belhaouane and his brother Mustafa guided the metamorphosis of their family mansion into Dar El Medina, the quarter's first boutique hotel. Rooms and suites range from over-the-top Ottoman to Moorish minimalist. At café tables by the courtyard fountain, well-dressed locals indulge in honey-drenched pastries and puff on tall silver *shishas,* or water pipes. Nearby is Dar El Jeld, another courtyard palace, given new life as one of the city's top restaurants, serving grilled fish with capers in a gorgeously tiled banquet hall.

But Tunis's cultural trove extends beyond the medina walls. The Bardo National Museum, housed in a 19th-century Hafside manse, has exhibitions for each civilization that prospered here: Carthaginian, Roman, Christian, Islamic, Jewish. Admiring its vast collection of Roman mosaics, you'll wonder why tourists haven't invaded as well, and you'll be glad you beat them to it. ✚

GUIDE, PAGE 275.

Doha

THE MIDDLE EAST'S NEXT CULTURAL CAPITAL?

Inside Doha's I. M.Pei-designed Museum of Islamic Art, above. Above left: A building created by Arata Isozaki for Education City. Opposite: A Qatari local in the newly renovated Souk Waqif.

ALONG THE CRESCENT bay in Doha, capital of the tiny Gulf emirate of Qatar, dozens of glittering new skyscrapers rise beside marble-lined shopping malls, luxury hotels, and waterfront apartment complexes meant to invoke the Italian Riviera. Just offshore, on its own man-made island, a stone-clad ziggurat floats above the blue waters of the gulf: the new Museum of Islamic Art, designed by I. M. Pei. The building's geometric structure incorporates so many distinguishing elements of Islamic architecture—carved stone, domes, arches, fountains, courtyards—that the effect is both archaic and intergalactic.

Once, this sun-scorched city was best known to Americans, if they were aware of it at all, as headquarters of the Al-Jazeera network. Now, with the country rich in petrodollars, Qatar's emir is reinventing its capital as the cultural hub of the Arab world, building schools and libraries, and making plans for several more museums. Education City, a palatial meta-university (many students arrive in chauffeur-driven cars; a placard instructs them to leave their maids outside) includes several American institutions. Qatar is still a conservative society—traditional robes and headdresses are the norm—but English is widely spoken, and visitors feel comfortable in Western clothing. Looking past Dubai's flash and glitz, Doha is evolving into a world-class city—with its roots still firmly in the shining desert sands. ✚

GUIDE, PAGE 275.

The dynamic streets of Ginza, one of Tokyo's best neighborhoods for shopping.

ASIA

NTT Do Co Mo
アートネイチャー
インド料理 NATARAJ
FOXEY ANNEX OFFICE
銀座五丁目

A Bo Peep–ready bodice at Metamorphose Harajuku, below. Right: The Mikimoto store in Tokyo's Ginza district. Opposite: Local resident Mitsuru Tanaka and a gaggle of high schoolers in Harajuku.

Tokyo

THE WORLD'S BEST BROWSING

STYLE INFORMS EVERY ASPECT of life in Japan's capital. This city is dead serious about fashion, so much so that visitors should set aside a day simply to check out what everyone is wearing. (Try not to gawk too openly.) The exquisite customer service in stores and the sheer range of offerings—from high-end to bargain-basement, traditional to groundbreaking—make Tokyo a fabulous place to shop. The challenge is trying to see it all, which is impossible, of course, but made easier by plentiful taxis and a willingness on the part of the general population to point you in the right direction. (Street addresses here are maddeningly vague.)

Start in the central Aoyama district, where Tokyo's home-grown stars—Issey Miyake, Yohji Yamamoto—as well as international heavy hitters have outposts. The clothes face heady competition from the buildings themselves, such as Chanel's Peter Marino–designed black-and-white cube and Jun Aoki's stacked-box venue for Louis Vuitton, both extraordinary >>

Shinjuku, the city's commercial center, above. Opposite, clockwise from top left: At Undercover, in Aoyama; Tokyoites in 80's-inspired looks; T-shirts at UES; a couple outside Laforet Harajuku.

visions of avant-garde design. Aoyama's new Omotesando Hills mall has every imaginable high-end shop, but also lesser-known wonders: Tabio offers a stunning array of socks, from polka-dotted whimsies to toeless multicolored knee-highs. In the same neighborhood you'll find Undercover, a temple for clothing that makes Comme des Garçons look like Ann Taylor: a chiffon jacket sprouts pink blossoms; a skirt is buried under a welter of crimson feathers.

The famed consumer thoroughfare of Ginza may lack the buzz of smaller neighborhoods, but any serious shopper will need at least one afternoon here. Wako is a classic department store with an elegant curved staircase and a surfeit of superb yet quiet merchandise, such as an exquisite skirt suit in apple-green silk. The Mikimoto Ginza store, designed by Toyo Ito & Associates, has a thrilling pearl-pink façade decorated with cutouts, and belies the jewelry firm's staid reputation.

Harajuku district, celebrated by everyone from John Galliano to Gwen Stefani, is Tokyo's hugely influential kiddyland, where throngs of outlandishly dressed teenagers parade their rebel chic. The store Metamorphose Harajuku is headquarters for the Lolitas, a now worldwide tribe of girls who get dolled up in tiny skirts distended by vast crinolines and patent shoes with bows. It's also fun to stroll by Laforet Harajuku, home to dozens of boutiques specializing in whatever is new (like fuzzy pink sweatshirts and matching pom-pom boots). Out front, patrons and wannabes congregate, insouciantly perched on the cutting edge. ✚

GUIDE, PAGE 277.

RACES
RIVET & REPAIR
BEST FOR GOODS

The main hall at Zenko-ji temple. Opposite, from left: Inside the Zawacc Caffé; Harue Watanabe, the mistress of Oyado Kinenkan.

Nagano

MODERNITY MEETS TRADITION IN THE JAPANESE ALPS

BEFORE 1988, this sleepy city in the foothills of the Japanese Alps was known chiefly for its seventh-century temple, Zenko-ji. Nagano was three hours by train from Tokyo, so visitors curled up for the night on futons in centuries-old *ryokan,* then rose to see the temple, ski in the surrounding mountains, and soak in one of the nearby *onsen,* or hot springs. Then came the Winter Olympics, the bullet train—and day trips.

Many inns disappeared, but there is at least one that is still worth a visit: the 200-year-old Oyado Kinenkan, in Daimon Minami. Its polished wood interior and sweet bean pastry–wielding *okami* (mistress) evoke a Japan that is rapidly disappearing.

For a modern treat, follow shop-lined backstreets to the Zawacc Caffé for pear caramel cake with ice cream, or fly along the ice like a gold medalist at the high-tech M-Wave skating arena. Then go to Zenko-ji, still Nagano's most thrilling site, and home of the first Buddhist statue brought to Japan (from Korea, in 552). In keeping with temple edict, the figure can never be seen—not even by the chief priest. But anyone can descend into a pitch-black tunnel and try to find the Key to Paradise, a lock on the wall near the hidden statue. Touch it and, so the rumor goes, you'll be granted enlightenment. ✚

GUIDE, PAGE 277.

A turreted corner of the Forbidden City. Opposite: Beijing's new Paul Andreu-designed National Grand Theater.

Beijing

A MONUMENTAL CITY'S OLYMPIAN EVOLUTION

THIS IS CHINA'S year of the City Transformed: the 2008 summer Olympics imposed a deadline on the lengthy remake of the nation's capital. Now manifest along the skyline are Herzog & de Meuron's bird's nest of a stadium; Paul Andreu's beehive-like national theater;

and the contorted arch of the Rem Koolhaas and Ole Scheeren-designed state television headquarters, the second-largest building in the world.

After the revolution of 1949, they say, Mao gazed down from the Gate of Heavenly Peace and announced that he wanted "the sky filled with smokestacks." Factories soon supplanted temples, gardens, and teahouses. Today, many Beijingers fear that their heritage is again on the chopping block. The idea of preservation is new here, and historic neighborhoods are under threat—but the Forbidden City, Summer Palace, and Temple of Heaven are being stunningly restored. Even as fresh marvels spring up, there's hope that the great ancient ones will stand reborn. ✚

GUIDE, PAGE 277.

T+L Tip

At the Beijing Planning Exhibition Hall, check out an extraordinarily detailed scale model of what the city aspires to look like by the year 2020.

Suzhou

THE ESSENTIAL DAY TRIP FROM SHANGHAI

MARCO POLO, in his 13th-century *Travels,* characterized Suzhou as the Venice of the East. Seven hundred years later, this city in the Yangtze River basin can still seem ages removed from the bustle of Shanghai, just a 60-minute train ride away. Suzhou draws visitors interested in seeing remarkably unscathed remnants of Old China: cobblestoned alleys, antique canals, bursts of wisteria. The 16th-century Garden for Lingering In has a covered walk that meanders through ginkgo groves, and pavilions that surround a pond famous for inspiring poetry.

But Suzhou is also a vital modern city. The area's ancient silk industry still thrives, and on factory tours you can see where the ethereal cocoons are made into butter-soft sheets. The metropolis has its share of semiconductor and iPod factories, too, and its newest star attraction is decidedly up-to-date: the I. M. Pei–designed Suzhou Museum, unveiled in 2006. Housing a fine collection of Chinese art and artifacts, from Ming scrolls to towering porcelain vases, Pei's structure, an angular masterpiece of skylights and white pagoda-like polygons, riffs on traditional Chinese architecture. The teahouse and garden are a minimalist take on the serene oases for which Suzhou has long been known. Just one more place for you to linger, and for future poets to describe. ✚

GUIDE, PAGE 278.

A window onto Suzhou's Garden for Lingering In. Opposite, from far left: The I. M. Pei–designed Suzhou Museum; at the Garden for Lingering In.

A boy navigates the watery approach to Thanjavur Palace's Arsenal Tower. Opposite, from left: Posing in DakshinaChitra, an artisans' community near Chennai; the bazaar in Tiruchirappalli, outside Madurai.

Tamil Nadu

IN A LAND OF EXTRAORDINARY TEMPLES

THE TEEMING, VIVID TEMPLE cities of India's southernmost state occupy an unfamiliar corner of the travel map. The agrarian pace of life here has not changed for centuries, though dynasties have come and gone—the Chola, the Pandya, the Vijayanagar—leaving behind a cultural heritage as opulent as any in Asia. Tamil Nadu's 50,000 square miles are mostly navigable by car, with distant points accessible by short plane rides.

Start in Chennai (formerly Madras), where the Government Museum is a little-visited attic of the Raj. Its collection of statuary is extraordinary, and includes many-armed Shivas from the Chola period, plus an 11th-century figure of the same god in his incarnation as the hermaphrodite Ardhanariswara. >>

Vishnu Temple, near Karaikudi, left. Opposite, clockwise from top left: The Krishna's Butterball rock, outside Chennai; the Chettinad Museum; Meenakshi Temple, in Madurai; a tonsured girl at Kundrakudi Temple, in Chettinad.

Then take a quick air hop to Madurai, a legendary seat of Hindu worship at least since the time of ancient Rome. The din of religious processions and ringing bells will fill your ears, and the sculptures of deities and erotic contortionists at the 16th-century Meenakshi Sundareswara temple (Madurai's most prominent landmark) will make your eyes pop.

Rent a car and circle through the nearby towns. Delightfully uncrowded Victorian museums are stocked with bronze dancing gods, and ancient temples are so thick on the ground that some have yet to be inventoried. The crumbling Palace Museum, in Thanjavur, has soaring ceilings, a vault shaped like a lotus flower, and perhaps the world's most important library of palm-leaf manuscripts.

Spend a few days in the Chettinad area. In the village of Karaikudi, the Bangala hotel has mottled terrazzo floors and rosewood doors, and the staff offer a warm, spontaneous welcome rarely encountered in this era of "guest relations." From here, you can range each day to the surrounding villages and explore the great Chettiar mansions, each more ornate than the next. The grand houses have scores of rooms, acres of tile roofs and marble floors, doors and pillars made from teak, and cornices inhabited by images not only of the goddess Meenakshi but also of helmeted British policemen. Like so much else in Tamil Nadu, they are among India's richest—and best hidden—treasures. ✚

GUIDE, PAGE 278.

Bangalore

WELCOME TO INDIA'S SILICON VALLEY

AROUND THE TURN of the millennium, at the height of Bangalore's high-tech boom, so much money and so many people flowed into this southern Indian metropolis that it felt like the city was being built in a day. Potholed roads were jammed with men on scooters, balancing computer monitors on helmetless heads, and office buildings grew at visible speed in seemingly every vacant lot. AT&T, Dell, and Citibank moved entire departments here.

Today, nearly a decade after Bangalore was anointed the ultimate symbol of globalization, outsourcing, and frictionless capitalism, it remains a work in progress, a symbol of how the future can announce its arrival—and then get called away on other business. But as Bangalore's growth rate has slowed, its mood has mellowed from pioneer hysteria to chic self-confidence. New shopping centers, nightclubs, and restaurants surround pockets of 19th- and early-20th-century colonial luxury. An ideal place from which to take it all in is the Park Bangalore, a Terence Conran–helmed boutique hotel. It's still Bangalore's moment—and the time to go is now. ✚

GUIDE, PAGE 278.

At the Park Bangalore hotel. Opposite, from far left: A roadside movie poster; on the campus of Infosys, a Bangalore-based IT consulting firm.

Jaisalmer

SONG FOR A DESERT STRONGHOLD

TO REACH THE ANCIENT CITADEL of Jaisalmer, in eastern Rajathstan, take a train from Jaipur, the state's seething capital. Journeying through the Thar Desert, you'll pass red dunes, mud huts with thatched roofs, and wild peacocks flashing like flamboyant roadrunners amid the scrub. Jaisalmer, a pale gold mass of buildings and fortifications, rises from the sands of the old Silk Road like a mirage. It is entered through a main gate that opens onto a

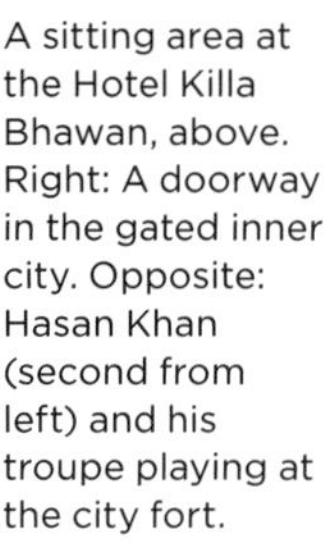
A sitting area at the Hotel Killa Bhawan, above. Right: A doorway in the gated inner city. Opposite: Hasan Khan (second from left) and his troupe playing at the city fort.

cobblestoned courtyard, across which loom the walls of the 12th-century inner city; intricately filigreed balconies, carved doors, and bell-shaped guard towers beckon.

The Killa Bhawan hotel is built into Jaisalmer's sandstone walls. Geometrically patterned dhurries deck the halls, saffron curtains envelop your canopy bed, pink pillows are piled on the wide divan.

Drop your bags and slip out again to wander the winding lanes below, where artisans sell garnet earrings and Mughal-style miniature paintings of demoiselle cranes. Squeezing through narrow alleys—past men in orange turbans, women in purple robes, and sacred cows—feels like something right out of *The Arabian Nights*. In the complex of linked Jain temples, one of Jaisalmer's architectural wonders, statues of the ancient religion's 24 prophets meditate with eyes and palms open.

For dinner, sample Rajasthani specialties at the restaurant on the crenellated roof of the Gorbandh Palace hotel, where Hasan Khan, the royal family's official musician, holds court. Accompanied by two of his sons, Khan and his harmonium create haunting melodies that bring to life the colors of an enchanted day. ✚

GUIDE, PAGE 278.

Bangkok

ROLLING DOWN THE RIVER OF KINGS

IN THAILAND, it always comes back to the river. For all Bangkok's trendy neighborhoods, grandiose shopping centers, and luxury hotels, the Chao Phraya, or River of Kings, remains the city's authentic heart. Slender long-tail boats, draped in ornate Buddhist garlands, deliver everything from passengers to fresh duck to bubbling noodle soups. Squat barges haul cement and tow logs. At the water's edge, Thais young and old go about their daily lives, swimming and washing and fishing. The Chao Phraya is a working river, bisecting one of Asia's most intense and exotic cities.

The best way to admire the crowded, captivating waterway is on a three-day cruise aboard the Manohra Dream, Bangkok's most lavish pleasure barge. Built on a century-old teak hull that once transported rice, it has two inviting air-conditioned staterooms with timber-paneled walls. The voyage begins in Bangkok and glides 45 miles north to Ayutthaya, the capital of ancient Siam until it was destroyed by Burmese invaders in 1767. Here, visitors can explore the magnificent ruins of Thai, Khmer, and Ceylonese temple compounds.

Those who prefer to sleep on terra firma can take one of several day cruises, or hop on a local commuter boat for less than $1. Alternatively, check into a waterside hotel. On the western bank, the Millennium Hilton and Peninsula Bangkok both have spacious rooms and spectacular river views. And at the eastern shore's 132-year-old Oriental (where rooms are swathed in Thai silks), one of the city's best breakfasts is served at the Verandah restaurant. As the sun ascends over the terrace, you can watch the river—and the city—come to life. ✚

GUIDE, PAGE 278.

The Rama VIII Bridge, spanning the Chao Phraya River.

Rai Lay

THE SEASIDE OF YOUR DREAMS—IN THAILAND

MANY BEACHES IN southern Thailand are overrun with Western travelers, but the quiet stretch of powdery sand known as the Rai Lay peninsula (or Rai Leh, or Railay) is an exception. These stark limestone cliffs and crystal blue Andaman Sea waters are a romantic alternative to crowd magnets like Phuket. What keeps the place secluded is its lack of easy access to the rest of the world: no roads lead to Rai Lay. To reach it, you first have to get to Krabi, an hour's flight from Bangkok or two hours' drive from Phuket, then catch a long-tail boat for a bouncy but exquisite 10-minute voyage. If you're staying at the Rayavadee resort, a speedboat will bring you to a 26-acre spread bordered by the sea on three sides, with two-level guest pavilions nestled in the jungle or perched over Phranang Beach. A simpler alternative can be found at the Sand Sea, in one of 68 bungalows just steps from the water.

You can walk between the peninsula's trio of beaches. Look for gibbons along the forest trail that winds toward a palm-fringed lagoon. Climbers should try scaling the headland's crags and pocked walls. The most inviting option: paddle the coast in a kayak. You'll discover sunken mangroves, even emptier beaches, and a cave dedicated to a princess goddess.

Afterward, relax with a massage, either the luxurious deep-tissue Thai Boran version at the Rayavadee or a $5 on-the-beach rubdown. Order *yum talay* (spicy seafood salad) or *chu chi goong* (prawns in red curry) at Krua Phranang. At sunset, sip cocktails at the Grotto, a bar tucked into a cliff.

And if you really want Rai Lay to yourself, visit between May and October, Thailand's monsoon season. Yes, it rains daily, but only in short, dramatic showers that keep down crowds and dust and turn the foliage an even deeper green. ✚

GUIDE, PAGE 279.

T+L Tip

Don't skip the fresh snacks hawked by locals right on the beach: satay *gai (grilled chicken skewers); spiky, lychee-like rambutans; and intensely sweet purple mangosteens.*

Sunset on Phranang Beach, above. Above right: Cooks at the Krua Phranang restaurant. Right: Pavilions at the Rayavadee resort. Opposite: A lagoon on the Rayavadee grounds.

Phnom Penh

PEACE AND SPLENDOR RETURN TO A GRAND SEAT OF CIVILIZATION

PHNOM PENH IS a place of extraordinary beauty: gold-leafed temple domes; eaves held up by mythical figures; houses on stilts; boats bobbing on the Mekong; giant heads carved in ancient stone in the style of Angkor Wat.

It is also a place of extraordinary human renewal. Just 30 years ago, the Khmer Rouge's genocide reduced Cambodia's capital to a ghost town. The terror that hung over Phnom Penh then is unimaginable. Now, on Monivong Boulevard—where the Khmer Rouge once entered the city—kids on scooters whiz past elegant hotels and restaurants. Tourists drink at riverside bars; families picnic on the grassy banks. Still, there is a strong note of melancholy. In the garden of the Tuol Sleng Genocide Museum, which is housed in a former prison, a respectful silence prevails.

Memories of the atrocities underscore this great city's rebirth. Phnom Penh today bursts with life. At the Russian Market you can find everything from 12th-century ceramics to a delicious, steaming bowl of noodles, chiles, and frog's legs. The old Hotel le Royal, restored by Raffles, is one of the most exquisite lodgings in Southeast Asia. The National Museum, next to the Royal Palace, displays magnificent sculptures from Angkor Wat, including a ninth-century statue of Shiva, Destroyer of Evil—who, it seems, has finally triumphed here. ✚

GUIDE, PAGE 279.

A Buddhist monk at the Tuol Sleng Genocide Museum, in a building that was once a Khmer Rouge stronghold, above right. Below right and opposite: Dance practice at Khmer Arts Academy.

Phu Quoc

A SLEEPING ISLAND BEAUTY WAKES UP

IF THERE'S A SYMBOL of the delicate equilibrium of Phu Quoc—of everything that's so alluring about this island off southwestern Vietnam—the Palm Tree must be it: an open-sided beach shack just yards from the surf, with 12 tables and red plastic chairs that sink into the sand. Mom cooks, daughter takes your order, son makes the drinks. The restaurant serves everything the day it's caught: squid, scallops, garrupa, kingfish. It's as humble as can be—and the food is fabulous.

The largest island in the Gulf of Thailand, 30-mile-long Phu Quoc is actually closer to Cambodia than to mainland Vietnam. Though it's just an hour by plane from Ho Chi Minh City,

Bai Sao, Phu Quoc's most popular beach, on the island's southeast coast. Opposite, clockwise from top right: grilled eggplant and local prawns at the Palm Tree; the pool at La Veranda Resort; a masseuse for hire on Bai Truong.

it has remained largely undeveloped. But it won't be for much longer. In 2004, Vietnam's prime minister ratified a proposal to develop Phu Quoc into a tourist destination, à la Phuket; since then, foreign corporations have pledged more than $6 billion toward luxury resorts and cruise-ship terminals, and an international airport is in the works.

For now, though, tourism here is just a trickle, supported by a small cluster of cafés and guest houses on Bai Truong, a 12-mile sweep of hourglass-fine sand on the east coast. Fortunately, one-third of the island—including 35,000 acres of primeval forest—is national parkland. Development has so far been confined to the northern end of Bai Truong, a pleasantly dizzy mile of thatched-roof *palapas*, concrete bungalows, seaside restaurants strung up with twinkly lights, and volleyball courts. Vietnamese women in indigo smocks and conical hats stroll the beach proffering pineapples, mangoes, and back rubs.

The island's red clay roads are trafficked mostly by tractors, >>

oxcarts, and the occasional hotel minivan; visitors get around by jeep or motorbike. The unofficial capital, Duong Dong, has the tumbledown aspect of a frontier town. At the daily market hundreds of vendors sell suckling pigs, fish just off the boat, and local produce, while a handful of seamstresses, shielded from the sun by pink parasols, work foot-cranked sewing machines.

Into this rustic scene has entered a surprisingly well-heeled guest: the $4.2 million Grand Mercure La Veranda Resort & Spa (which opened on Bai Truong in August 2006), no doubt the vanguard of what's to come. With just 43 rooms on 2.5 acres, it's no sprawling mega-resort, but among the simple bungalows and cottages that flank it (the Palm Tree is just next door), La Veranda sticks out like a triple-tiered wedding cake in a breadbasket. The look is cheery French colonial: pastel walls, terra-cotta tiles, whitewashed louvers, paddle fans stirring the air. And the setting is pure tropical bliss.

That such a gorgeous and untrammeled island as this could still exist seems a minor miracle, especially in Southeast Asia, where one is forever hearing about some bygone golden age. From Ko Chang to Ko Lanta, Lombok to Luang Prabang, the refrain's the same: Should have been here 10 years ago. Well, in Phu Quoc, at this moment, it is 10 years ago. ✚

GUIDE, PAGE 279.

The daily market in Duong Dong. Opposite, clockwise from far left: One of La Veranda's guest rooms; grill-it-yourself squid at the restaurant Gio Bien; Nguyen Thi Xuan Chau, the spa receptionist at La Veranda.

A view of the Tasman Sea, near Scamander, in Tasmania.

AUSTRALIA + NEW ZEALAND + THE SOUTH PACIFIC

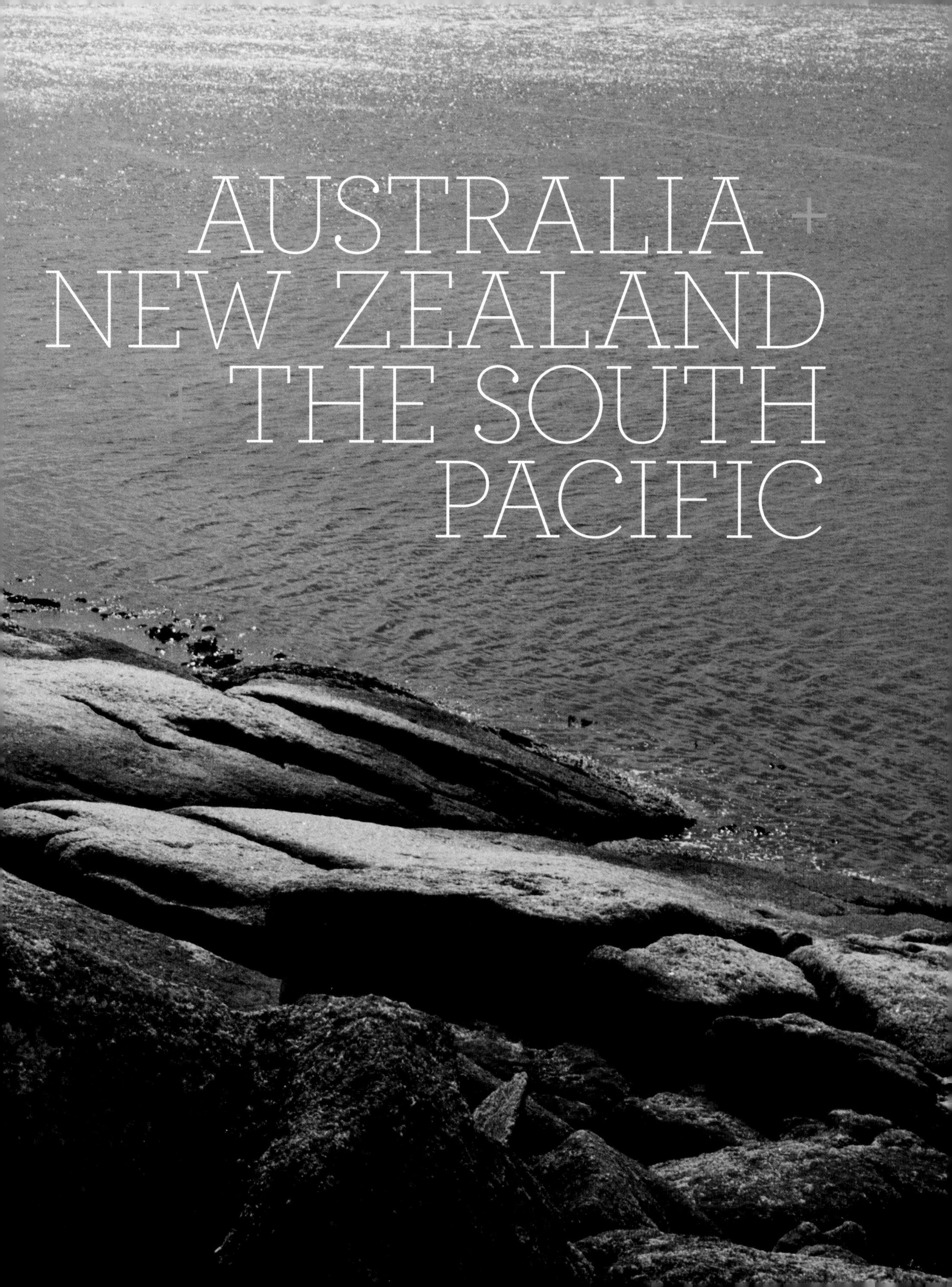

Sydney

SAVORING FAR EAST FLAVORS DOWN UNDER

IN A CITY SO BLESSED by climate and geography, hyperbole comes naturally. And to the long list of Sydney superlatives, add this: dish for dish, it has the finest Asian food on the planet. No other city—not Singapore, not Hong Kong, not Bangkok—offers such assured cooking or such a wide range of cuisines.

Why? Immigrants from East and Southeast Asia have formed a major demographic in Australia for more than a century, and in Sydney they have access to superb ingredients—fabulously fresh organic produce, renowned Australian beef and lamb, and seafood from the Sydney Fish Market, the world's second largest, after Tokyo's.

The results can be found at a tiny Thai canteen named Spice I Am. The 20-seater has no proper chairs, no liquor license, not even a front wall. What it does offer is no-holds-barred Thai cooking: *pla tod ka min*, deep-fried whiting nuanced with turmeric and coriander, and *hoy tod*, a savory crêpe filled with luscious briny mussels that you never dreamed you'd taste outside of southern Thailand.

In Chinatown's crowded alleys, Cantonese food was once the only option. Today there's an explosion of regional fare. Chinese Noodle Restaurant's specialty is the hearty dishes of the north. Through the kitchen window watch owner Qan Xiao Tang make his famous wheat noodles, unfurling and beating out great strands of dough. >>

The kitchen staff at Yoshii. Opposite, from far left: *Pla tod ka min* (deep-fried whiting) at Spice I Am; Sydney's famed harbor and opera house.

Ichi-ban Boshi, in the Galeries Victoria mall. Opposite, clockwise from top left: Duck with cinnamon at Billy Kwong; chefs at Spice I Am; Yoshii's egg custard; roast poultry and sausages at Tai Wong.

Down the street at Tai Wong, lacquered ducks, geese, and quail are lined up like Rockettes on skewers. Beyond rough-and-tumble Chinatown is chic Billy Kwong, where the draw is comfort food built from organic, sensitively raised ingredients. This must be the only Chinese restaurant on earth that serves biodynamic eggs.

In the vibrant suburb of Cabramatta, an uncanny simulacrum of Saigon, potted mandarin trees and herbal apothecaries line the sidewalks. Inside Thanh Binh, the menu lists no fewer than 251 dishes. But don't skip the *pho* (beef noodle soup): its stock—spiced with star anise, cardamom, and cloves—simmers for 26 hours.

For Sunday-morning dim sum (called *yum cha*) Sydneysiders head for aircraft-hangar-sized palaces like Marigold Citymark, where waiters in tuxedos pour jasmine tea with a flourish and dour ladies circulate steam trolleys. Malaya, the granddaddy of Sydney's Asian hot spots, is where many Australians first sampled chilies, *galangal,* and lemongrass. Order the creamy, piquant *laksa,* a magnificent Malaysian king prawn soup. And Ichi-ban Boshi, a modest noodle shop in a tony Japanese mall, turns out the city's best *tantanmen*—ramen laden with minced pork and scallions.

Few tourists have heard of Yoshii, but this six-year-old Japanese gem might be the finest restaurant in all of Australia. Chef Ryuichi Yoshii is a culinary art-house director, his mesmerizing 17-course *omakase* a daring drama. Act I, Scene 1: an eggshell in a silver cup, containing silky custard, snow-pea chiffonade, bonito broth, and rich sea urchin ornamented with gold leaf. The next 16 dishes build excitement like a fireworks display, leading to a denouement fit for a Sydney cook's tour. ✚

GUIDE, PAGE 281.

TAI 12 WONG BARBEQ

Great Alpine Road

HEAD FOR THE HILLS IN VICTORIA

IN JANUARY, DURING Melbourne's searing summer, the mercury shoots past 110 and curbside trees look ready to burst into flame. Cool off by following the Great Alpine Road into Victoria's mountainous terrain. Three hours northeast of the city, at Myrtleford, vineyards start to flash green between leafy towns, and the air begins to feel fresh. Stop for the night in Bright and check into a chalet at the Buckland Studio Retreat. Dine at Simone's—Melbourners make the trip for chef Patrizia Simone's risotto-stuffed zucchini blossoms alone.

From there, detour along an unpaved road that plunges from a landscape of granite into lush snow-gum forest. In urbane Falls Creek, the apartment-hotel Huski resort has a well-regarded spa and a groovy stacked-cube façade.

The next day press on to Omeo, a historic mining town, keeping an eye out for the century-old Blue Duck Inn as you make your way. Its crusty bread and trout-leek soup are the country lunch you dream of—and rarely find.

Reconnect with the Great Alpine Road in Omeo and loop back up through Bright, where you can veer off on a route that climbs through scented eucalyptus groves into the Snowy Mountains, Australia's highest range. The best spot for lunch is in Khancoban, at Crackenback Farm & Cottage, a restaurant with vaulted ceilings, linen-covered tables, and perfectly tart lemonade. ✚

GUIDE, PAGE 281.

Huski resort, in Falls Creek. Opposite, from far left: Koala crossing near the Great Alpine Road; the Ovens River, near Bright, in northern Victoria.

At Lebrina, in Hobart, left. Above: Oysters at Apsley Gorge vineyard. Opposite: A view of the Derwent River from the vineyard Moorilla.

Tasmania

SMALL ISLAND, BIG DELICACIES

A TINY FRUIT FARM in Scamander, a half-mile from the Tasmanian coast, is stocked with all things berry—jams, chutneys, ice cream—and has a sign that promises an array of bests. The sign doesn't lie. The strawberries, piercingly sweet, are easily the finest you have ever tasted; so is the summer pudding. Credit the wind for the sophisticated food and wine culture of an island once considered a backwater. It whips around the globe before pounding Tasmania, leaving the soil and surrounding waters some of the least contaminated on the planet. Even in Hobart, Tasmania's capital (an ideal base for a tour of Australia's smallest state), the air smells of foxgloves and sweet alyssum. And in the wild congeries of microclimates—a two-hour drive can encompass white-sand beaches, coastal lagoons, lush pastureland, and primeval forest—you can grow, harvest, or extract almost anything: stone fruits, truffles, Wagyu >>

The entrance to Eureka Farm, in Scamander, right. Opposite, clockwise from top left: Hobart's harbor; a dairy farm in northeast Tasmania; Frogmore Creek's winemaker, Tony Scherer; zucchini and cauliflower salad at Lebrina.

beef, rock oysters, not to mention leatherwood honey, which, drawn from the dense rain forest, might be the most delicious substance of all.

Chef Scott Minervini deftly exploits this cornucopia at Lebrina, his Hobart restaurant, in dishes such as kingfish topped with piquant fresh garlic shoots, the first caught and the second grown just a few stone's-throws away. At Daniel Alps's fine restaurant in Rosevears, about three hours to the north, the larder is stocked with organic herbs and vegetables untouched by any hands but the cooks'. Says Alps, "I couldn't live in a place where I couldn't see the ingredients I work with growing around me."

But the most ambitious expression of the Tasmanian food philosophy is the restaurant Peppermint Bay. To get there, board a deluxe catamaran in Hobart Harbor and cruise up the Derwent River, past the occasional pod of migrating whales. The voyage is an appropriate warm-up for marine delights like tartare of cured ocean trout with capers, crème fraîche, and trout crisp.

Tasmania's winemakers are all about artisanal production, too. Savor the results at Moorilla, on the Derwent River, not far from Hobart, or at Frogmore Creek, just south of the city. At Apsley Gorge, winemaker (and former abalone diver) Brian Franklin crafts a gorgeous Pinot Noir in a repurposed fish factory. And in summer, he'll catch and grill you a seafood feast that you'll wish would never end. ✚

GUIDE, PAGE 281.

T+L Tip
Pack a copy of A Guide to Tasting Tasmania, *by Graeme Phillips. Its the definitive resource for the island's food scene.*

South Island

NEW ZEALAND'S BACK OF BEYOND

WITH JUST 30,000 INHABITANTS, the South Island's west coast makes Australia's outback seem crowded. It's not a brochure destination: the towns seem as though trapped in amber; it rains a lot; there are none of the lavish lodges for which the Kiwis are famous. Yet its landscapes (and seascapes) are among the most spectacular and diverse in the Southern Hemisphere.

Take Fox Glacier , a river of ice cutting west toward the Tasman Sea. You can view it by helicopter, but try hiking the rain forest and climbing down directly onto this frigid fantasyland. Nearby is Lake Matheson, where reflections of lofty Mount Cook shine through wisps of fog on the water's crystal surface.

Drive north on Highway 6 along the gloriously deserted coast, and stay the night just inland at Lake Brunner Lodge, built in the 1930's and powered by a waterfall. Next day, head to Punakaiki Pancake Rocks, eerie stacks of limestone shaped by crashing waves, and Cape Foulwind, home to seals—and, at the Bay House, famous seafood chowder.

Continue north on State Highway 67 to the Rough & Tumble Bush Lodge, a riverside inn with views of the Glasgow Ranges. At full flood, you can fish off the veranda; just grab a rocking chair and wait for the water to rise. ✚

GUIDE, PAGE 281.

Punakaiki Pancake Rocks, on the South Island's west coast. Opposite: Eight-mile-long Fox Glacier.

A sitting room at Whare Kea Lodge. Opposite: The lodge's solitary alpine chalet.

Wanaka

A FAVORITE NEW KIWI GETAWAY

ANYONE WHO'S SEEN a *Lord of the Rings* film has already fallen in love with Lake Wanaka. The craggy snow-capped peaks that rim its expanse are familiar to fans as Tolkien's Misty Mountains. Such outrageously scenic surroundings, along with world-class skiing and renowned local wineries, explain why Wanaka has been grabbing nearby Queenstown's mantle as the South Island getaway of choice.

You can drive to Wanaka from that larger, more famous rival in roughly 45 minutes, along the highest main road in New Zealand. A breathtaking zigzag climb through the Crown Range Pass brings you to rolling hills spiked with speargrass, then to tiny Cardrona, where you can lunch on excellent pub grub at the town's 1863 Cardrona Hotel, under the eye of the dusty wild boar mounted above the fireplace.

Fifteen miles on is Wanaka itself. Cafés and a couple of very fine bottle shops occupy the burg's small center, which runs right down to the lake. Arrive in January or February, and you'll discover that the summertime activities here—canyoneering, jet boating, tandem paragliding—are as thrilling as winter's black diamond chutes.

Wanaka doesn't yet have Queenstown's plethora of flash accommodations, but lakeside Whare Kea Lodge, with room for 12 guests, offers Kiwi luxury at its understated best. Each suite has drop-away mountain and water views, and the staff can supply a guide, equipment, and a driver for any adventure. Or stay in Whare Kea's lone mountain chalet—accessible only by helicopter—for alpine picnics, meandering walks, and unrivaled privacy. Be alert for Gandalf sightings. ✚

GUIDE, PAGE 281.

Society Islands

THE SOUTH SEAS IN THE WAKE OF GAUGUIN

TAHITI: THE MERE mention of the word, long a synonym for tropical paradise, sets the mind adrift on a turquoise lagoon fringed by coco palms and scarlet hibiscus. Today, French Polynesia's main island is a stopover for travelers en route to one of the other 117, which retain the grace and beauty that entranced Paul Gauguin.

The group's second most popular isle, Moorea, rises from the ocean like a glorious green cathedral. In the shadow of its peaks, a coast road curls past plain white churches and silvery pineapple fields. Visit one of the motu (islets) that surround it. Motu Fareone has snorkeling, swimming, and the idyllic Villa Corallina. Or boat to Moea to lunch on spicy prawn curry at La Plage café and watch kite surfers dance on the water. Many travelers head to tiny Bora-Bora, where the motu are dotted with luxe overwater-bungalow resorts such as St. Regis, and Orient-Express's Bora Bora Lagoon & Spa.

Henri Matisse discovered his Eden in the Tuamotu Archipelago's coral atolls. One, Fakarava, austerely beautiful rather than lush, is part of a UNESCO nature reserve renowned for world-class diving. Swimming its light-filled lagoon is like gliding through an infinite mirror. ✚

GUIDE, PAGE 281.

Overwater bungalows at the St. Regis Bora-Bora.

UNITED STATES + CANADA

THE GUIDE

PROVINCETOWN, MA

WHERE TO STAY

Race Point Lighthouse Restored keeper's house and outbuilding at an 1876 Cape Cod lighthouse. 508/487-9930; racepoint lighthouse.net; keeper's house doubles from $$; Whistle House (sleeps eight) $$$$$ per week.

WHERE TO EAT

Ciro & Sal's Northern Italian food prepared with local ingredients. 4 Kiley Court; 508/487-6444; dinner for two ●●●.

Clem & Ursie's A don't-miss raw-bar happy hour. 85 Shank Painter Rd.; 508/487-2333; dinner for two ●●.

WHAT TO SEE & DO

Art's Dune Tours SUV-rides along the Cape Cod National Seashore. 4 Standish St.; 508/487-1950; artsdunetours.com.

Flyer's Boat Rental Powerboats, kayaks, and sailboats; lessons available. 131A Commercial St.; 508/487-0898; flyers boatrentals.com.

Ptown Bikes The town's best selection of rentable bicycles. 42 Bradford St.; 508/487-8735; ptownbikes.com.

Whydah Museum Artifacts from a 1717 pirate ship that wrecked just off the coast. MacMillan Wharf; 508/487-8899; whydah.com.

MONADNOCK REGION, NH

WHERE TO STAY

E. F. Lane Hotel 40 smartly decorated rooms in a renovated 1890 brick department store. 30 Main St., Keene; 888/300-5056 or 603/357-7070; eflane.com; doubles from $$.

Inn at Valley Farms Antiques-filled B&B in a 1774 Colonial house, surrounded by organic gardens. 633 Wentworth Rd., Walpole; 877/327-2855 or 603/756-2855; innatvalleyfarms.com; doubles from $$.

WHERE TO EAT

L.A. Burdick Provençal cooking, and trademark housemade chocolate desserts. 47 Main St., Walpole; 603/756-2882; dinner for two ●●●●.

WHAT TO SEE & DO

Colonial Theatre Landmark venue showcasing plays, live music, and films. 95 Main St., Keene; 603/357-1233; thecolonial.org.

Keene Pumpkin Festival Annual October extravaganza that celebrates all things pumpkin. 603/358-5344; pumpkinfestival.org.

VERMONT

WHERE TO STAY

Pitcher Inn Historic, graceful hostelry near Sugarbush Resort. 275 Main St., Warren; 888/867-4824 or 802/496-6350; pitcherinn.com; doubles from $$$.

Stowe Mountain Lodge Timber-and-stone resort completed in June 2008, at the base of the ski hill. 7412 Mountain Rd., Stowe; 888/478-6938 or 802/253-3560; stowe mountainlodge.com; doubles from $$$.

Topnotch Resort & Spa 120-acre retreat with a Nordic center and an excellent spa. 4000 Mountain Rd., Stowe; 800/451-8686 or 802/253-8585; topnotchresort.com; doubles from $$$.

Twin Farms Lavish and sprawling rustic-chic spread. Royalton Tpk., Barnard; twinfarms.com; 800/894-6327 or 802/234-9999; doubles from $$$$$, all-inclusive.

WHERE TO SHOP

Barnard General Store Open since 1832. 6134 Route 12, Barnard; 802/234-9688.

Warren Store Specialty grocer downstairs, clothing and toy shop upstairs. 284 Main St., Warren; 802/496-3864.

WHERE TO SKI

Stowe Mountain Resort Straddles Vermont's highest peak and has a new base village. 5781 Mountain Rd., Stowe; 800/253-4754; stowe.com.

Sugarbush Resort 111 powdery trails and a terrain park—alongside a newly updated inn, lodge, and base village. 1840 Sugarbush Access Rd., Warren; 800/537-8427; sugarbush.com.

BROOKLYN

WHERE TO STAY

Bowery Hotel 135 rooms, many with city views, near the New Museum of Contemporary Art. 335 Bowery, Manhattan; 212/505-9100; theboweryhotel.com; doubles from $$$.

Hotel on Rivington Downtown hipster beacon sheathed in glass. 107 Rivington St., Manhattan; 800/915-1537 or 212/475-2600; hotelonrivington.com; doubles from $$$.

WHERE TO EAT

Frankies 457 Spuntino Sublime Italian restaurant with an of-the-moment vibe. 457 Court St., Carroll Gardens; 718/403-0033; dinner for two ●●●.

Franny's Fabulous and inventive brick-oven pizzas. 295 Flatbush Ave., Prospect Heights; 718/230-0221; dinner for two ●●.

Good Fork Korean-meets-French food. 391 Van Brunt St., Red Hook; 718/643-6636; dinner for two ●●.

Peter Luger New York's best straight-ahead

KEY

LODGING

- under $150 = **$**
- $150–$299 = **$$**
- $300–$699 = **$$$**
- $700–$999 = **$$$$**
- $1,000 + up = **$$$$$**

DINING

- under $25 = ●
- $25–$74 = ●●
- $75–$149 = ●●●
- $150–$299 = ●●●●
- $300 + up = ●●●●●

porterhouse. 178 Broadway, Williamsburg; 718/387-7400; dinner for two ●●●.

WHERE TO SHOP

Bird Popular boutique that stocks denim by Sass & Bide and dresses by 3.1 Phillip Lim. 430 Seventh Ave., Park Slope, 718/768-4940; 220 Smith St., Carroll Gardens, 718/797-3774.

Future Perfect Top-notch design shop. 115 N. Sixth St., Williamsburg; 718/599-6278.

Sleep High-end lingerie. 110 N. Sixth St., Williamsburg; 718/384-3211.

NIGHTLIFE

Barbès The live-music roster at this club runs the gamut from washboard swing to klezmer. 376 Ninth St., Park Slope; 718/965-9177.

Bar Tabac Excellent bistro and watering hole with a friendly, neighborhood feel. 128 Smith St., Cobble Hill; 718/923-0918.

Jalopy Theater Great venue for country blues and folk music, next to the shipping docks. 315 Columbia St., Columbia Waterfront District; 718/395-3214.

Zebulon Showcases some of the city's best jazz and Afrobeat musicians—every night, for free. 258 Wythe Ave., Williamsburg; 718/218-6934.

PHILADELPHIA

WHERE TO STAY

Sheraton Society Hill Right next to Third Street shopping. 1 Dock St.; 800/325-3535 or 215/238-6000; starwood.com; doubles from $$$.

WHERE TO EAT

Continental For martinis and tapas. 138 Market St.; 215/923-6069; dinner for two ●●.

Fork Acclaimed restaurant with a menu featuring local ingredients. 306 Market St., 215/625-9425; dinner for two ●●●.

WHERE TO SHOP

Bruges Home Two-story design studio carrying everything from coffee-table books to club chairs. 323 Race St.; 215/922-6041.

Deep Sleep Menswear shop with the latest street styles. 54 N. Third St.; 215/351-9124.

Reform Vintage Modern A favorite professional dealers' source for Midcentury furniture. 112 N. Third St.; 215/922-6908.

Third Street Habit Top indie-designer labels, and great sales. 153 N. Third St.; 215/925-5455.

Vagabond Cutting-edge women's boutique that helped jumpstart Old City's fashion renaissance. 37 N. Third St.; 267/671-0737.

NORTHERN VIRGINIA

WHERE TO STAY & EAT

Clifton Inn 18-room hotel with classic country charm and an excellent restaurant. 1296 Clifton Inn Dr., Charlottesville; 888/971-1800 or 434/971-1800; cliftoninn.net; doubles from $$; dinner for two ●●●.

Keswick Hall Laird-of-the-manor grandeur and some of Virginia's most compelling seasonal food. 701 Club Dr., Keswick; 800/274-5391 or 434/979-3440; keswick.com; doubles from $$$; dinner for two ●●●.

WHAT TO SEE & DO

Chrysalis Vineyards Known for their bottles of Petit Manseng; cook out on the property's iron grills. 23876 Champe Ford Rd., Middleburg; 540/687-8222.

International Gold Cup and Virginia Gold Cup Steeplechase races held each October and May, respectively. Great Meadow, 5089 Old Tavern Rd., The Plains; 540/347-1215; vagoldcup.com.

Kluge Estate Terrific sparkling wines and a David Easton-designed tasting room. 3550 Blenheim Rd., Charlottesville; 434/984-4855.

CUMBERLAND ISLAND, GA

WHERE TO STAY

Greyfield Inn 10-room getaway on a former Carnegie family estate. 866/401-8581; greyfield inn.com; doubles from $$$, including ferry transfers.

TRANSPORT

National Park Service Ferry For day trips from St. Mary's, Georgia; island bike rentals are also available through the Park Service. 912/882-4335; nps.gov.

VERO BEACH, FL

WHERE TO STAY

Disney's Vero Beach Resort Inspired by grand Victorian-era seaside hotels, but with all the contemporary bells and whistles. 9250 Island Grove Terrace; 407/939-7540; disneybeachresorts.com; doubles from $$$.

Driftwood Inn Rambling beach house turned hotel with two ocean-view pools. 3150 Ocean Dr.; 772/231-0550; thedrift wood.com; doubles from $.

WHAT TO SEE & DO

McKee Botanical Garden Native and exotic plants, plus lots of scurrying lizards. 350 U.S. Hwy. 1; 772/794-0601; mckee garden.org.

SEASIDE, FL

WHERE TO STAY

Dreamland Heights Comfortable and conveniently located rental condos. 121 Central Sq., Seaside; 800/277-8696 or 850/231-2222; cottage rentalagency.com; doubles from $$.

Hotel Saba Poolside cabanas and 56 guest rooms, slated to open early this year. 63 Main St., Rosemary Beach; 866/854-7222 or 850/278-7222; doubles from $$$.

Inn by the Sea, Vera Bradley Nine rooms, designed by the handbag tycoon Barbara Bradley Baekgaard. 2311 E. Country Rd., Seaside; 800/358-8696; innbytheseavb.com; doubles from $$.

WHERE TO EAT

Bud & Alley's The spot for locally caught seafood, with a popular roof-deck bar. 2236 County Rd. 30A, Seaside; 850/231-5900; dinner for two ●●●.

Onano Neighborhood Café Convivial Italian bistro. 78 Main St., Rosemary Beach; 850/231-2436; lunch for two ●●●.

NEW ORLEANS

WHERE TO STAY

International House Intimate, welcoming hotel with a happening bar. 221 Camp St.; 800/633-5770 or 504/553-9550; ihhotel.com; doubles from $$.

Ritz-Carlton 1909 Beaux Arts building with a new spa, on the edge of the French Quarter. 921 Canal

St.; 800/241-3333 or 504/524-1331; ritzcarlton.com; doubles from $$$.

WHERE TO EAT

Café Minh Vietnamese and French flavors, joined to winning effect. 4139 Canal St.; 504/482-6266; dinner for two ●●.

Cochon A hearty Cajun menu: crawfish pie, the namesake roast pig. 930 Tchoupitoulas St.; 504/588-2123; dinner for two ●●.

Domilise's Some of the city's best po' boys. 5240 Annunciation St.; 504/889-9126; dinner for two ●●.

Franky & Johnny Another top po' boy spot. 321 Arabella St.; 504/899-9146; dinner for two ●●.

Lüke Rattan chairs, belt-cranked fans, and a classic European menu. 333 St. Charles Ave.; 504/378-2840; dinner for two ●●●.

Napoleon House Landmark famed for its Pimm's Cup and jambalaya. 500 Chartres St.; 504/524-9752; lunch for two ●●.

WHAT TO SEE & DO

Grayline New Orleans Bus tours pass by a breached levee and through the Lower Ninth Ward. 504/569-1401; graylineneworleans.com.

St. Bernard Project Non-profit that assigns volunteers to house-rebuilding sites for stints of a day or more. 504/277-6831; stbernardproject.org.

NIGHTLIFE

Vaughan's Down-home bar with great live jazz. 800 Lesseps St.; 504/947-5562.

DALLAS

WHERE TO STAY

Belmont Hotel Freshly renovated 1946 hotel. 901 Fort Worth Ave.; 866/870-8010 or 214/393-2300; belmontdallas.com; doubles from $.

Hotel Palomar Chic property with a central location. 5300 E. Mockingbird Lane; 800/597-8399 or 214/520-7969; kimptonhotels.com; doubles from $$$.

Rosewood Mansion on Turtle Creek Legendary hotel that has long been one of the city's best; in the midst of a $20 million renovation. 2821 Turtle Creek Blvd.; 888/767-3966 or 214/559-2100; mansiononturtlecreek.com; doubles from $$$.

WHAT TO SEE & DO

Dallas Museum of Art Century-old institution with wide-ranging collections. 1717 N. Harwood; 214/922-1200; dallasmuseumofart.org.

Dallas Center for the Performing Arts Norman Foster- and Rem Koolhaas-designed opera and theater venues, slated to open this year. 2106 Boll St.; 214/954-9925; dallasperformingarts.org.

Morton H. Meyerson Symphony Center I. M. Pei–designed concert hall. 2301 Flora St.; 214/670-3600; meyersymphonycenter.com.

Nasher Sculpture Center Calder, Miró, Ernst, and a beautiful oak-filled garden. 2001 Flora St.; 214/242-5100; nashersculpturecenter.org.

HAMILTON COUNTY, IN

WHERE TO STAY

Conner Prairie Frontier history museum, with family weekend overnights three times a year. 13400 Allisonville Rd., Fishers; 800/966-1836 or 317/776-6000; connerprairie.org; two-day stay for a family of four $$$$, including meals.

CHICAGO

WHERE TO STAY

The James Minimalist rooms with high-tech amenities. 55 E. Ontario St.; 877/526-3755 or 312/337-1000; jameshotels.com; doubles from $$.

Peninsula Chicago Excellent service and location. 108 E. Superior St.; 866/288-8889 or 312/337-2888; peninsula.com; doubles from $$$.

WHERE TO EAT

Hot Doug's Sophisticated sausages. 3324 N. California Ave.; 773/279-9550.

Murphy's Red Hots Perfectly cooked Vienna beef dogs. 1211 W. Belmont Ave.; 773/935-2882.

Superdawg Drive-In Carside service and a retro vibe. 6363 N. Milwaukee Ave.; 773/763-0660.

Wiener's Circle Outside the city, but worth the trek. 2622 N. Clark St.; 773/477-7444.

Wolfy's Featured in *While You Were Sleeping*. 2734 W. Peterson Ave.; 773/743-0207.

MONTANA

WHERE TO STAY

Lodgepole Gallery & Tipi Village Blackfoot-tribe tipi camp just outside Glacier National Park. 406/338-2787; blackfeetculturecamp.com; two-night packages from $$$, including meals and entertainment.

LAS VEGAS

WHERE TO STAY

Flamingo Las Vegas Opened by Bugsy Siegel in 1946, and still a hot spot. 3555 Las Vegas Blvd. S.; 800/732-2111; flamingolasvegas.com; doubles from $.

The Platinum A new addition to the Strip area, with a rooftop pool. 211 E. Flamingo Rd.; 877/211-9211; theplatinumhotel.com; doubles from $$.

WHERE TO EAT

Bartolotta Ristorante di Mare Bi-level dining room with lakeside loggias and fresh Mediterranean fish. 3131 Las Vegas Blvd. S.; 702/770-3305; dinner for two ●●●●.

Bubble Bar at Restaurant Guy Savoy 20-seat boîte serving small plates and champagne by the glass. 3570 Las Vegas Blvd. S.; 877/346-4642; dinner for two ●●●.

NIGHTLIFE

Blush Celeb-heavy spot with a lantern-lit dance floor. 3131 Las Vegas Blvd. S.; 702/770-3633.

VAIL, CO

WHERE TO STAY

Arrabelle at Vail Square 36-room hotel that ups the area's posh level, steps

KEY

LODGING

under $150 = **$**
$150–$299 = **$$**
$300–$699 = **$$$**
$700–$999 = **$$$$**
$1,000 + up = **$$$$$**

DINING

under $25 = ●
$25–$74 = ●●
$75–$149 = ●●●
$150–$299 = ●●●●
$300 + up = ●●●●●

from Vail's Eagle Bahn gondola. 675 Lionshead Place; 866/662-7625 or 970/754-7777; arrabelle.com; doubles from $$$$.
Tivoli Lodge 40-year-old mainstay, recently refreshed. 386 Hanson Ranch Rd.; 800/451-4756 or 970/476-5615; tivolilodge.com; doubles from $$$.
Vail Plaza Hotel & Club Just-opened Alpine-inspired property in the village. 16 Vail Rd.; 877/888-1540 or 970/477-8000; vailplazahotel.com; doubles from $$$.

WHERE TO SKI

Vail Resort Vast and varied terrain; legendary back bowls. 450 E. Lionshead Circle, Vail; 877/204-7881; vail.com.

SANTA FE, NM

WHERE TO STAY

El Rey Inn Lovingly maintained Route 66 landmark. 1862 Cerrillos Rd.; 800/521-1349 or 505/982-1931; elreyinnsantafe.com; doubles from $.
Inn of the Anasazi, A Rosewood Hotel A showcase for the Santa Fe look (handwoven rugs, kiva-shaped fireplaces), steps from the plaza. 113 Washington Ave.; 800/688-8100 or 505/988-3030; innoftheanasazi.com; doubles from $$$.

WHAT TO SEE & DO

James Kelly Contemporary Lauded gallery exhibiting international artists. 1601 Paseo de Peralta; 505/989-1601; jameskelly.com.
Museum of Spanish Colonial Art Extensive collections housed in a historic Pueblo Revival building. 750 Camino Lejo; 505/982-2226; spanishcolonial.org.
Robert Nichols Gallery Devoted almost exclusively to clay-based work. 419 Canyon Rd.; 505/982-2145; robertnicholsgallery.com.
Santa Fe Railyard Sprawling new complex of museums, galleries, and performance spaces. 332 Read St.; 505/982-3373; sfrailyardcc.org.
Site Santa Fe Cutting-edge arts nonprofit that hosts a renowned biennial. 1606 Paseo de Peralta; 505/989-1199; sitesantafe.org.

WHERE TO SHOP

Seret & Sons For one-of-a-kind Afghani textiles and Tibetan antiques. 224 Galisteo St.; 505/988-9151.

PHOENIX

WHERE TO STAY

Hotel Valley Ho Retro-cool 50's-era classic. 6850 E. Main St., Scottsdale; 866/882-4484 or 480/248-2000; hotelvalleyho.com; doubles from $$.
Four Seasons Resort Pueblo-inspired complex adjacent to a high-desert nature preserve. 10600 E. Crescent Moon Dr.; 800/332-3442 or 480/515-5700; fourseasons.com doubles from $$$.

LAKE POWELL, AZ + UT

WHERE TO STAY

Lake Powell Resort 350-room hotel with panoramic lake views. 100 Lakeshore Dr., Page, AZ; 800/528-6154 or 928/645-2433; lakepowell.com; doubles from $$.
Wahweap Marina The best place for houseboat rentals. 100 Lakeshore Dr., Page, AZ; 800/528-6154; lakepowell.com; rentals from $$$$$ for three days.

CULVER CITY, CA

WHERE TO STAY

Culver Hotel 1920's Renaissance-Revival property. 9400 Culver Blvd.; 310/838-7963; culverhotel.com; doubles from $$.

WHAT TO SEE & DO

Billy Shire Fine Arts Outsider-art gallery. 5790 Washington Blvd.; 323/297-0600; billyshirefinearts.com.
Blum & Poe Well-regarded gallery with a stable of prominent contemporary artists. 2754 S. La Cienega Blvd.; 310/836-2062; blumandpoe.com.
Gregg Fleishman Studio Geometric furniture and objets. 3850 Main St.; 310/202-6108; greggfleishman.com.
Kirk Douglas Theatre Acclaimed plays presented by the Center Theatre Group. 9820 Washington Blvd.; 213/628-2772; centertheatregroup.org.
Museum of Design Art and Architecture Diverse shows explore the play between art and architecture. 8609 Washington Blvd.; 310/558-0902; modaagallery.com.

WHERE TO SHOP

Denizen Design Gallery Cutting-edge furniture and housewares. 8600 Venice Blvd.; 310/838-1959.

SAN FRANCISCO

WHERE TO STAY

Hotel Triton Eco-minded property, down to the enviro-friendly wall paint and organic cotton bedsheets. 342 Grant Ave.; 800/800-1299 or 415/394-0500; hoteltriton.com; doubles from $$.
Orchard Garden Hotel Among the country's first LEED-certified hotels, a quick walk from Union Square. 466 Bush St.; 888/717-2881 or 415/399-9807; theorchardgardenhotel.com; doubles from $$.

WHERE TO EAT

Café Gratitude A local vegan chain that's the antithesis of McDonald's. 2400 Harrison St.; 415/824-4652; lunch for two ••.
Farmer Brown Locavore soul food. 25 Mason St.; 415/409-3276; dinner for two ••.
Yield Wine Bar Rotating wine list and small-plates menu. 2490 Third St.; 415/401-8984.

WHAT TO SEE & DO

California Academy of Sciences A planetarium, natural history museum, aquarium, and "rain forest" in a stunning Renzo Piano-designed building. Golden Gate Park; 415/379-8000; calacademy.org.
De Young Museum Extensive collections, now housed in a Herzog & de Meuron structure. 50 Hagiwara Tea Garden Dr., Golden Gate Park; 415/750-3600; deyoungmuseum.org.
Flora Grubb Gardens Forward-thinking plant store and coffee bar. 1634 Jerrold Ave.; 415/648-2670.
S.F. Recycling & Disposal Inc. The inspired city dump features a hilltop sculpture garden and quarterly artist-in-residence exhibitions.

501 Tunnel Ave.; 415/330-1415; sfrecycling.com.

TRANSPORT

EV Rental Cars Local chain with a fleet of eco-friendly vehicles. 877/387-3682; evrental.com.

PORTLAND, OR

WHERE TO STAY

Ace Hotel 79-room spot with vintage touches and contemporary decor, next to the Pearl District. 1022 SW Stark St.; 503/228-2277; acehotel.com; doubles from $.

Jupiter Hotel Stylish converted motel. 800 E Burnside St.; 877/800-0004 or 503/230-9200; jupiterhotel.com; doubles from $.

WHERE TO EAT

Voodoo Doughnut Innovative flavors with quirky names like Grape Ape and Butter Fingering. 22 SW Third Ave.; 503/241-4704.

WHERE TO SHOP

Alma Chocolate Handmade fair-trade chocolates. 140 NE 28th Ave.; 503/517-0262.

WHAT TO SEE & DO

Burnside Skatepark One of the best skateboarding parks in the world. Under the east end of the Burnside Bridge.

Japanese Garden In a city of beautiful gardens, this is among the prettiest. 611 SW Kingston Ave., Washington Park; 503/223-1321; japanesegarden.com.

NIGHTLIFE

The Alibi An ode to the tiki bar. 4024 N Interstate Ave.; 503/287-5335.

Doug Fir Lounge Modernist log cabin with great live shows. 830 E Burnside St.; 503/231-9663.

PAIA, HI

WHERE TO STAY

Mama's Fish House Nine light-filled cottages with covered lanais on Kuau Cove. 799 Poho Place; 808/579-9764; mamasfishhouse.com; doubles from $$.

Hawaii's Best Rentals Condos, cottages, and villas to let, many on the beach. 866/772-5642; hawaiisbestrentals.com.

WHERE TO EAT

Anthony's Coffee Co. Breakfast central. 90 Hana Hwy.; 808/579-8340

Mama's Fish House An oceanside institution; make reservations. 799 Poho Place; 808/579-8488; dinner for two ●●●●.

Mana Foods Health-food store with great prepared dishes. 49 Baldwin Ave; 808/579-8078.

KAUAI, HI

WHERE TO STAY

Grand Hyatt Kauai Resort & Spa Sprawling, partially solar-powered 602-room retreat, with extensive gardens. 1571 Poipu Rd., Koloa; 800/233-1234 or 808/742-1234; hyatt.com; doubles from $$$.

Hanalei Bay Resort Hillside property with spectacular ocean views. 5380 Honoiki Rd., Princeville; 800/827-4427 or 808/826-6522; hanaleibayresort.com; doubles from $$.

WHAT TO SEE & DO

Outfitters Kauai Local tour company offering zip-line safaris and kayak-ing expeditions. 2827A Poipu Rd., Poipu; 808/742-9667; outfitterskauai.com.

NORTH HATLEY, QUEBEC

WHERE TO STAY & EAT

Manoir Hovey Romantic lakeside inn with an upscale-Québécois restaurant. 575 Chemin Hovey; 800/661-2421 or 819/842-2421; manoirhovey.com; doubles from $$$, including dinner.

WHAT TO SEE & DO

Route Verte Quebec's extensive network of biking trails. routeverte.com.

St.-Benoît-du-Lac Benedictine monastery with apple orchards. Chemin Fisher, St.-Benoît-du-Lac; 819/843-4080; st-benoit-du-lac.com.

WHERE TO SHOP

LeBaron Grocery 120-year-old general store with locally made cheeses. 105 Main St.; 819/842-2487.

MONTREAL

WHERE TO STAY

Hôtel Gault 30-room property with vividly hued, contemporary interiors, in a historic downtown building. 449 Rue Ste.-Hélène; 866/904-1616 or 514/904-1616; hotelgault.com; doubles from $$.

WHERE TO EAT

Joe Beef Friendly bistro with an oyster bar and extensive Québécois menu. 2491 Rue Notre-Dame Ouest; 514/935-6504; dinner for two ●●●.

WHAT TO SEE & DO

Belgo Building Former garment factory now houses dozens of galleries and studios. 372 Rue Ste.-Catherine Ouest; 514/861-0305.

WHERE TO SHOP

Couleurs Meubles et Objéts du 20e Siècle Specializes in Midcentury wares. 3901 Rue St.-Denis; 514/282-4141.

Philippe Dubuc Expertly tailored men's suits. 4451 Rue St.-Denis; 514/282-1465.

NIGHTLIFE

Bílý Kůň Low-key craft-beer bar. 354 Mont-Royal Est; 514/845-5392.

Pop! Bar à Vin Wine bar with a Scandinavian bent. 250 Pine Ave. Est; 514/287-1648.

CHILKO LAKE, BRITISH COLUMBIA

WHERE TO STAY

Lodge at Chilko Lake Timber lodge surrounded by guest cabins. Chilko-Newton Rd.; 888/639-1114 or 250/229-2115; chilkolake.com; three-night packages from $$$$$, including meals, activities, and air transfers from Vancouver.

KEY

LODGING

under $150 = **$**
$150–$299 = **$$**
$300–$699 = **$$$**
$700–$999 = **$$$$**
$1,000 + up = **$$$$$**

DINING

under $25 = ●
$25–$74 = ●●
$75–$149 = ●●●
$150–$299 = ●●●●
$300 + up = ●●●●●

PUERTO RICO
VIRGIN GORDA
ST. JOHN
SABA
NEVIS
DOMINICA

CARIBBEAN + BERMUDA

DOMINICA

WHERE TO STAY

Exotica Cottages Mountain retreat with seven cabins and an organic café. Giraudel; 767/448-8839; exotica-cottages.com; doubles from $.

Jungle Bay Resort & Spa Cliffside wooden cottages and two yoga studios. Pointe Mulâtre; 767/446-1789; junglebaydominica.com; doubles from $$$, all-inclusive.

3 Rivers Eco Lodge Bungalows and tree houses—largely solar-energy powered—in a valley. Rosalie; 767/446-1886; 3riversdominica.com; doubles from $.

NEVIS

WHERE TO STAY

Four Seasons Resort Gingerbread-trimmed buildings next to Pinney's Beach. Charlestown; 800/332-3442 or 869/469-1111; fourseasons.com; doubles from $$$.

Montpelier Plantation Inn 17 elegant, airy rooms on a historic estate. St. John's Parish; 869/469-3462; montpeliernevis.com; doubles from $$.

WHAT TO SEE & DO

Culturama Annual independence celebration, held each July, with parades, concerts, and calypso competitions. nevisculturama.net.

Museum of Nevis History Local artifacts housed in a replica of island native Alexander Hamilton's birthplace. Low St., Charlestown; 869/469-5786.

SABA

WHERE TO STAY

Gate House Cozy hillside hideaway with a five-room inn and two private villas. Hell's Gate; 877/456-5198 or 011-599/416-2416; sabagatehouse.com; doubles from $.

House on the Path Restored clapboard cottage in the rain forest, a quick stroll from town. Windwardside; 011-599/580-9188; houseonthepath.com; doubles from $$.

Queen's Gardens Resort The island's most luxurious option: 12 roomy suites with panoramic views. Troy Hill; 011-599/416-3494; queensaba.com; doubles from $$.

ST. JOHN

WHERE TO STAY

Caneel Bay, A Rosewood Resort 166 tropical-posh guest rooms in a former Rockefeller estate, surrounded by beaches. North Rd., Cruz Bay; 888/767-3966 or 340/776-6111; caneelbay.com; doubles from $$$.

Maho Bay Camps Pioneering eco-resort: simple jungle tents connected by elevated boardwalks. Cruz Bay; 800/392-9004 or 340/715-0501; mahobay.org; doubles from $.

WHERE TO EAT

Woody's Seafood Saloon Excellent conch fritters. Cruz Bay; 340/779-4747; dinner for two ●.

VIRGIN GORDA

WHERE TO STAY

Biras Creek Light-filled suites on a secluded peninsula. North Sound; 800/223-1108 or 284/494-3555; biras.com; doubles from $$$, including meals.

Bitter End Yacht Club Watersports-centric beachfront resort. North Sound; 800/872-2392 or 305/468-0168; beyc.com; doubles from $$$$, including meals.

Rosewood Little Dix Bay Storied former Rockefeller property, recently overhauled. The Valley; 888/767-3966 or 284/495-5555; littledixbay.com; doubles from $$$$.

WHERE TO EAT

Sugar Mill Haute-Caribbean cooking at Little Dix Bay resort. The Valley; 284/495-5555; dinner for two ●●●●.

WHERE TO SHOP

Buck's Market The place for picnic staples. Virgin Gorda Yacht Harbor; 284/495-5423.

Thee Artistic Gallery Island-inspired jewelry and accessories. Spanish Town; 284/495-5104.

PUERTO RICO

WHERE TO STAY

Hacienda Gripiñas Charming inn on a former coffee plantation. 144 Crta. Estatal, Jayuya; 787/828-1717; haciendagripinas.com; doubles from $, including dinner.

Horned Dorset Primavera Luxe beachside resort. Km 3, Crta. 429, Rincón; 800/633-1857 or 787/823-4030; horneddorset.com; doubles from $$$.

WHERE TO EAT

Mark's Top-notch Puerto Rican–influenced cooking at a family-run hotel. 75 Cristina, Ponce; 787/284-6275; dinner for two ●●●.

Restaurant Aaron Horned Dorset Primavera's French-Caribbean restaurant. Km 3, Crta. 429, Rincón; 787/823-4030; dinner for two ●●●.

WHAT TO SEE & DO

Acampa Nature Adventures Guided hikes in the Reserva Forestal Toro Negro. 787/706-0695; acampapr.com.

Rincón Surf School Lessons for all levels. Hwy. 413, Barrio Puntas, Rincón; 787/823-0610; rinconsurfschool.com.

BERMUDA

WHERE TO STAY

Cambridge Beaches Perennial favorite, recently refreshed. 30 Kings Point Rd., Sandys; 800/468-7300 or 441/234-0331; cambridgebeaches.com; doubles from $$$.

Elbow Beach Old-school classic with a stylish new look. 60 South Shore Rd., Paget; 800/223-7434 or 441/236-3535; mandarinoriental.com; doubles from $$$.

The Reefs Revered by its repeat guests; with an expanded spa and two restaurants. 56 South Shore Rd., Southhampton; 800/742-2008 or 441/238-0222; thereefs.com; doubles from $$$.

MEXICO + CENTRAL + SOUTH AMERICA

SAYULITA, MEXICO

WHERE TO STAY

Les Oiseaux Volants Ecclectic seven-bedroom villa. 4A Calle Delfin; 52-329/291-3468; lovesayulita.com; from $$$$$.

Petit Hotel d'Hafa Friendly inn near the sea. 55 Avda. Revolución; 52-329/291-3806; sayulitalife.com; doubles from $.

WHERE TO EAT

Choco Banana For breakfast burritos. 14 Calle Delfin; 52-329/291-3051.

Sayulita Fish Taco Fried seafood and to-die-for salsa. 13 José Mariscal; 52-329/291-3272.

WHERE TO SHOP

Pachamama Well-edited boutique. 4B Calle Delfin; 52-329/291-3468.

MICHOACÁN, MEXICO

WHERE TO STAY

Hotel Don Bruno Simple rooms; a pretty courtyard. 92 Morelos, Angangueo; 52-715/156-0026; doubles from $.

OAXACA, MEXICO

WHERE TO STAY

Camino Real Hotel Former convent with lush courtyards. 300 Calle Cinco de Mayo; 52-951/501-6100; camino-real-oaxaca.com; doubles from $$.

RIVIERA MAYA, MEXICO

WHERE TO STAY

Azul Beach Hotel Secluded oceanfront compound. Crta. Cancún-Puerto Morelos; 52-998/872-8080; karismahotels.com; from $$, all-inclusive.

Hotel Esencia Tranquil estate with guest rooms and cottages. Crta. Cancún-Tulum; 877/528-3490 or 713/528-7862; hotelesencia.com; doubles from $$$.

WHAT TO SEE & DO

Hidden Worlds Swimmable cave pools. 52-984/877-8535.

Xcaret Water park plus live shows. Crta. Chetumal-Puerto Juárez; 52-998/883-0470.

Xel-Ha Eco-conscious water park. Crta. Chetumal-Puerto Juárez; 52-998/884-9422.

NOSARA, COSTA RICA

WHERE TO STAY

Harmony Hotel Elegant, simple lodge. 506-2/682-4114; harmonynosara.com; doubles from $$.

Hotel Lagarta Lodge 12-person cabin on a nature reserve. 506-2/682-0035; lagarta.com; doubles from $.

WHAT TO SEE & DO

Nosara Boat Tours For fishing trips. 506-2/682-0610; nosaraboattours.com.

CARTAGENA, COLOMBIA

WHERE TO STAY

Casa Pestagua 17th-century manse. 33-63 Santo Domingo; 57-5/664-9510; casapestagua.net; doubles from $$$.

Hotel Charleston Cartagena Lovely rooms, rooftop pool. Plaza de Santa Teresa; 57-5/664-9494; hotelescharleston.com; doubles from $$$.

El Marqués Hotel Boutique In a converted colonial house. 33-41 Santo Domingo; 57-5/660-0746; elmarqueshotelboutique.com; doubles from $$.

Hotel Agua Bright, six-room spot. 4-29 Ayos; 57-5/664-9479; hotelagua.com.co; doubles from $$$.

WHERE TO EAT

8-18 Caribbean fare. 2-124 Gastelbondo; 57-5/664-2632; dinner for two ●●●.

Palma South American dishes. 38-137 Curato; 57-5/660-2796; dinner for two ●●.

Restaurante La Vitrola The place to be seen. 2-01 Baloco; 57-5/664-8243; dinner for two ●●●.

NIGHTLIFE

Café Havana Popular dance hall. At Media Luna and Guerrero; 57-315/690-2566.

Quiebra Canto Lively salsa joint. Parque Centenario; 57-5/664-1372.

LAKE TITICACA, PERU + BOLIVIA

WHERE TO STAY

All Ways Travel For homestays. 51-51/353-979; titicacaperu.com; doubles from $.

Inkaterra Titilaka Stylish new lodge on a remote peninsula. 800/442-5042; inkaterra.com; doubles from $$$$, all-inclusive.

CASABLANCA VALLEY AND SAN ANTONIO, CHILE

WHERE TO STAY

Matetic Guesthouse Century-old estancia. Fundo el Rosario, Casablanca; 56-2/232-3134; mateticvineyards.com; doubles from $$$.

WHERE TO EAT

House of Morandé Assured, contemporary food. Ruta 68, Casablanca; 56-32/275-4701; lunch for two ●.

Indómita Nuevo-Chilean cooking. Ruta 68, Casablanca; 56-32/275-4400; lunch for two ●●.

WHAT TO SEE & DO

Garcés Silva One of the region's first vineyards. Fundo San Andrés de Huinca, San Antonio; 56-2/428-8080.

Veramonte Winery with 1,100 acres of vines. Ruta 68, Casablanca; 56-32/232-9924.

BUENOS AIRES, ARGENTINA

WHERE TO STAY

Home Hotel Chic rooms in Palermo Viejo. 5860 Calle Honduras; 54-11/4778-1008; homebuenosaires.com; doubles from $.

WHERE TO SHOP

Arandú Leather handicrafts. 1924 Ayacucho; 54-11/4800-1575.

Gil Antigüedades Vintage clothing. 412 Humberto I; 54-11/4361-5019.

Lucila Iotti Cutting-edge shoe boutique. 2212 Malabia; 54-11/4833-0206.

Mariano Toledo Clothes by a local designer. 1450 Armenia; 54-11/4137-7777.

Perez Sanz One-of-a-kind accessories. 1477 Posadas; 54-11/4812-1417.

LAKE DISTRICT, ARGENTINA

WHERE TO STAY

Correntoso Lake & River Hotel Luxe fishing camp. Villa La Angostura; 54-11/4803-0030; correntoso.com; doubles from $$.

Llao Llao Hotel & Resort Mountaintop lodge. Bariloche; 54-2944/448-530; llaollao.com; doubles from $$$.

WHERE TO EAT

Hamburguesería Peperone Great burgers. San Martín; 54-2997/422-296.

KEY

LODGING

under $150 = $
$150–$299 = $$
$300–$699 = $$$
$700–$999 = $$$$
$1,000 + up = $$$$$

DINING

under $25 = ●
$25–$74 = ●●
$75–$149 = ●●●
$150–$299 = ●●●●
$300 + up = ●●●●●

WESTERN EUROPE

LONDON

WHERE TO STAY

Main House Eclectically decorated, stylish B&B in a Notting Hill townhouse. 6 Colville Rd.; 44-20/7221-9691; themainhouse.co.uk; doubles from $$.

Milestone Hotel Sumptuous red-brick Victorian property opposite Kensington Palace. 1 Kensington Court; 800/223-6800 or 44-20/7917-1000; milestonehotel.com; doubles from $$$.

WHERE TO EAT

The Ebury Two-story gastropub near Sloane Square. Pimlico Rd.; 44-20/7730-6784; dinner for two ●●●.

Fino Upscale Soho tapas restaurant. 33 Charlotte St.; 44-20/7813-8010; dinner for two ●●●.

The Ledbury Wunderkind Brett Graham's homage to classic French cooking. 127 Ledbury Rd.; 44-20/7792-9090; dinner for two ●●●●.

Notting Hill Brasserie Neighborhood spot with an inventive menu. 92 Kensington Park Rd.; 44-20/7229-4481; dinner for two ●●●●.

Odette's Modern British food in a revamped classic space. 130 Regents Park Rd.; 44-20/7586-8569; dinner for two ●●●●.

Theo Randall at the InterContinental Italian dishes made with English produce by a River Café alum. 1 Hamilton Place; 44-20/7318-8747; dinner for two ●●●.

Trinity Refined yet hearty cooking served in a walnut-paneled room. 4 The Polygon; 44-20/7622-1199; dinner for two ●●●.

The Waterway Burgers, steaks, and Sunday barbecues, plus a terrace over the Grand Union Canal. 54–56 Formosa St., Little Venice; 44-20/7266-3557; dinner for two ●●●.

BRIGHTON, ENGLAND

WHERE TO STAY

Blanch House Townhouse hotel with cheeky but sophisticated interiors. 17 Atlingworth St.; 44-1273/603-504; blanchhouse.co.uk; doubles from $$.

Drakes Posh 20-room seaside inn. 43–44 Marine Parade; 44-1273/696-934; drakesofbrighton.com; doubles from $$.

WHERE TO EAT

Blanch House Innovative food prepared with locally sourced ingredients; the stark-white dining room is equally hip. 17 Atlingworth St.; 44-1273/603-504; dinner for two ●●●.

The Forager Expertly prepared pub-food classics. 3 Stirling Place, Hove; 44-1273/733-134; dinner for two ●●●.

WHAT TO SEE & DO

Brighton Museum Idiosyncratic holdings range from 19th-century children's blocks to a Salvador Dalí couch. Royal Pavilion Gardens; 44-1273/292-882; brighton.virtualmuseum.info.

Royal Pavilion 1820's palace that is a riot of Orientalist fantasia—minarets, domes, gilded dragons. Open daily for tours. Steine Gardens; 44-1273/292-822; royalpavilion.org.uk.

LIVERPOOL, ENGLAND

WHERE TO STAY

Hope Street Hotel Airy, light-filled rooms in a century-old brick building. 40 Hope St.; 44-151/709-3000; hopestreethotel.co.uk; doubles from $$.

The Malmaison Sumptuous hotel with Gothic-inspired interiors. 7 William Jessop Way, Princes Dock; 44-151/229-5000; malmaison-liverpool.com; doubles from $$$.

WHERE TO EAT

London Carriage Works Paul Askew's ambitious French-English restaurant. 40 Hope St.; 44-151/705-2222; dinner for two ●●●.

Philharmonic Pub Ornate pub with Art Deco touches, once a Beatles' favorite. 36 Hope St.; 44-151/707-2837; dinner for two ●●.

WHAT TO SEE & DO

The Bluecoat Legendary gallery and performance space. School Lane, 44-151/709-5297; thebluecoat.org.uk.

Everyman Theatre New plays, often by local writers. 13 Hope St.; 44-151/708-3700; everymanplayhouse.com.

Liverpool Playhouse Theater classics performed in a 19th-century music hall. 13 Hope St.; 44-151/708-3700; everymanplayhouse.com.

Tate Liverpool Converted-warehouse branch of the London museum. Albert Dock, 44-151/702-7400; tate.org.uk.

Walker Art Gallery Small but impressive collections, from medieval book panels to David Hockney paintings. William Brown St., 44-151/478-4199; liverpoolmuseums.org.uk.

WALES

WHERE TO STAY & EAT

Bell at Skenfrith Cozy inn with inspired, season-driven food. Skenfrith, Monmouthshire; 44-160/075-0235; skenfrith.co.uk; doubles from $$; dinner for two ●●●.

Felin Fach Griffin Popular hotel-restaurant that put Wales on the gourmet map. Felon Fach Brecon, Powys; 44-187/462-0111; eatdrinksleep.ltd.uk; doubles from $$; dinner for two ●●●.

Llys Meddyg Georgian carriage house turned hostelry, with an innovative restaurant. East St., Newport, Pembrokeshire; 44-123/982-0008; llysmeddyg.com; doubles from $$; dinner for two ●●●.

THE LOWLANDS, SCOTLAND

WHERE TO STAY

Glenapp Castle Restored 17-room castle with extensive grounds, overlooking the Irish Sea. Ballantrae, Ayrshire; 44-14/6583-1212; glenappcastle.com; doubles from $$$$, including dinner.

Kirroughtree House Stately manor with an

KEY

LODGING

under $150 = **$**
$150–$299 = **$$**
$300–$699 = **$$$**
$700–$999 = **$$$$**
$1,000 + up = **$$$$$**

DINING

under $25 = ●
$25–$74 = ●●
$75–$149 = ●●●
$150–$299 = ●●●●
$300 + up = ●●●●●

oak-paneled lounge. Newton Stewart, Wigtownshire; 44-16/7140-2141; kirrough treehouse.co.uk; doubles from $$, including dinner.

WHAT TO SEE & DO

Auchentoshan Distillery Producers of a rare triple-distilled whisky; tours available. A82 by Dalmvir, Clydebank; 44-13/8987-8561; auchentoshan.co.uk.

Bladnoch Distillery Riverside outfit with a weekend Whisky School; tours available. Wigtown; 44-19/8840-2605; bladnoch.co.uk; Whisky School $1,000 per person, including some meals.

Glenkinchie Distillery Scotland's largest stills and a whisky-making exhibit, just outside Edinburgh; tours available. Pentcaitland, East Lothian; 44-18/7534-2004; malts.com.

COUNTY CORK, IRELAND

WHERE TO STAY

Ballyvolane House Elegant but informal 1728 manor. Castlelyons, Fermoy; 353-25/36349; ballyvolanehouse.ie; doubles from $$$.

Glengarriff Lodge Eight-person thatch-roofed house on a private river island. Glengarriff; 353-27/63833; glengarriff-lodge.com; weekly rates from $$$$$.

Maritime Hotel Trim new business hotel on Bantry Bay. The Quay, Bantry; 353-27/54700; themaritime.ie; doubles from $$.

WHERE TO EAT

Ballymaloe House Brought Irish farmhouse cooking into the international limelight. Shanagarry; 353-21/464-6785; dinner for two ●●●●.

Ballyvolane House Four-course menus that reflect the local harvests. Castlelyons, Fermoy; 353-25/30349; dinner for two ●●●●.

Farmgate Café Short, excellent menu of hearty dishes, in Cork City's bustling English Market. Grand Parade, Cork City, 353-21/427-8134; lunch for two ●●●●.

Fishy Fishy Café Down-to-earth seafood house featuring the day's fresh catch. Pier Rd., Kinsale; 353-21/470-0415; lunch for two ●●●.

Gleeson's Restaurant The menu lists the local farm from which each ingredient hails. 3 Connolly St., Clonakilty; 353-23/21834; dinner for two ●●●.

Good Things Café Slate tables, Philippe Starck-designed chairs, and deeply flavorful dishes. Ahakista Rd., Durrus; 353-27/61426; dinner for two ●●●●.

Moran's Oyster Cottage *The* place for Galway Bay oysters, for more than 200 years. The Weir, Kilcolgan; 353-91/796-113; dinner for two ●●●.

WHAT TO SEE & DO

Ballymaloe Cookery School Culinary classes at the famed restaurant-hotel. Shanagarry; 353-21/464-6785; cookingisfun.ie.

WHERE TO SHOP

Manning's Emporium Well-stocked shop with artisanal West Cork cheeses. Ballylickey, Bantry; 353-27/50456.

Rory Connor For handmade knives. Ballylickey, Bantry; 353-27/50032; by appointment.

NIGHTLIFE

An Teach Beag Pub where local musicians play every night. 2 Quay St., Galway; 353-91/539-897.

ANDALUSIA, SPAIN

WHERE TO STAY

Casa Morisca Hotel Converted 15th-century townhouse with Moorish-style interiors and views of the Alhambra. 9 Cuesta de la Victoria, Granada; 34/958-221-100; hotelcasa morisca.com; doubles from $$.

Casa Rural El Olivar Farmhouse B&B owned by Belgian expats. 6 Cierzos y Cabreras, Iznájar; 34/95-753-4928; casaruralel olivar.com; doubles from $.

Hospes Las Casas del Rey de Baeza Renovated 18th-century monastery with a courtyard and a rooftop pool. 2 Plaza Jesús de la Redención, Sevilla; 34/95-456-1496; hospes.es; doubles from $$$.

WHERE TO EAT

Restaurante La Finca The place for top-notch paella, in the countryside just outside Granada. Carr. Salinas-Villaneuva Tapias, KM 65.5; 34/95-832-1861; dinner for two ●●●●.

Restaurante Ruta del Azafrán Known for grilled bacalao with Moroccan spices. 1 Paseo de los Tristes; 34/95-822-6882; dinner for two ●●●.

Taberna Salinas For regional dishes such as serrano suckling pig. 3 Tundidores, Córdoba; 34/95-748-0135; dinner for two $$.

WHAT TO SEE & DO

El Centro Cultural Cajasol Excellent flamenco shows, especially on Thursday nights. 4 Laraña, Seville; 34/95-450-8200.

SAN SEBASTIÁN, SPAIN

WHERE TO STAY

Hotel Iturregi Eight luxe but simple rooms in a hillside fishing village. Barrio Azkizu; 34/94-389-6134; hoteliturregi.com; doubles from $$$.

Villa Soro Stylish 19th-century estate. 61 Avda. Ategorrieta; 34/94-329-7970; villasoro.com; doubles from $$$.

WHERE TO EAT

Arzak Updated tavern atmosphere with cutting-edge food. 273 Avda. Alcalde Elosegui; 34/94-327-8465; dinner for two $$$$$.

Martín Berasategui Three Michelin stars and a marathon, Basque-inspired tasting menu. 4 Calle Loidi, Lasarte-Oria; 34/94-336-6471; dinner for two $$$$$.

San Prudencio Low-key Basque cooking. Getaria; 34/94-314-0627; dinner for two $$$.

PARIS

WHERE TO STAY

Hôtel Le Sainte-Beuve On the Left Bank, with 22 individually decorated rooms. 9 Rue Ste-Beuve, 6th Arr.; 33-1/45-48-20-07; hotel-sainte-beuve.fr; doubles from $$.

Le Général Hôtel Hip yet inviting, with sleek all-white bathrooms and a green apple on every bed pillow. 5–7 Rue Rampon, 11th Arr.; 33-1/47-00-41-57; legeneralhotel.com; doubles from $$$.

WHERE TO EAT

Café des Deux Moulins Stars as itself in the movie *Amélie*. 15 Rue Lepic, 18th Arr.; 33-1/42-54-90-50; dinner for two ●●●.

Le Laffitte Dedicated to the classics, like pork shoulder with lentils and chocolate mousse. 43 Rue Laffitte, 9th Arr.; 33-1/42-80-07-66; dinner for two ●●●.
Le Pure Café A *très* cool vibe, and an enormous horseshoe-shaped zinc bar. 14 Rue Jean Macé, 11th Arr.; 33-1/43-71-47-22; dinner for two ●●●.
Mélac Bistrot à Vins Specializes in dishes from the Auvergne. 42 Rue Léon Frot, 11th Arr.; 33-1/43-70-59-27; dinner for two ●●●.

BORDEAUX, FRANCE

WHERE TO STAY

Château Cordeillan-Bages Chic rooms in an 18th-century former monstery. Rte des Châteaux, Pauillac; 800/735-2475 or 33-5/56-59-24-24; cordeillanbages.com; doubles from $$.
Château les Merles Updated country house with a nine-hole golf course. Tuilières, Mouleydier; 33-5/53-63-13-42; lesmerles.com; doubles from $$.
Château Rigaud Owned by a young British couple and often filled in part by their *confrères*. Mouliets et Villemartin; 33-5/57-40-78-59; chateaurigaud.co.uk; doubles from $$$.
La Maison Bord'eaux City-center B&B with fresh interiors. 113 Rue du Dr. Albert Barraud, Bordeaux; 33-5/56-44-00-45; lamaisonbord-eaux.com; doubles from $$$.

WHERE TO EAT

Le Petit Commerce Relaxed and popular seafood bar. 22 Rue du Parlement St.-Pierre, Bordeaux; 33-5/56-79-76-58; dinner for two ●●●.
Thierry Marx Acclaimed molecular gastronomy in the Médoc. Château Cordeillan-Bages, Rte des Châteaux, Pauillac; 33-5/56-59-24-24; dinner for two ●●●●●.

WHAT TO SEE & DO

Château Beychevelle Sprawling winery surrounded by perfectly manicured gardens. St.-Julien-Beychevelle; 33-5/56-73-20-70.
École du Vin Wine-country tours and on-site tasting courses. 1 Cours du XXX Juillet, Bordeaux; 33-5/56-00-22-85; ecole.vins-bordeaux.fr.
Wine Tours with James Bonnardel Private excursions, customized by a local oenologist. 33-8/72-25-17-89.

ÎLE DE RÉ, FRANCE

WHERE TO STAY

Le Corps de Garde Former watchhouse with a casual, beachy feel. 1 Quai Clemenceau, St.-Martin-de-Ré; 33-5/46-09-10-50; lecorpsdegarde.com; doubles from $$.

WHERE TO EAT

Au Bord d'un Zinc Great for fresh seafood. Place du Marché, St.-Martin-de-Ré, Île de Ré; 33-6/88-96-84-46; dinner for two ●●●.
L'Avant Port Elegant boîte that serves *vanet*, a local scallop-like shellfish. 8 Quai Daniel Rivaille, St.-Martin-de-Ré; 33-5/46-68-06-68; dinner for two ●●●●.

AVEYRON, FRANCE

WHERE TO STAY

Le Comptoir d'Aubrac Designer Catherine Painvin's lovely inn. Aubrac; 33-5/65-48-78-84; catherinepainvincouture.com; doubles from $$.
Hôtel-Restaurant Bras Minimalist glass-walled hotel. Rte. de l'Aubrac, Laguiole; 33-5/65-51-18-20; michel-bras.com; doubles from $$$.
Hôtel-Restaurant Château de Creissels A 12th-century manse with rooms overlooking the Millau Viaduct. Rte. de St.-Afrique, Millau; 33-5/65-60-16-59; chateau-de-creissels.com; doubles from $.

WHERE TO EAT

Hôtel-Restaurant Bras For chef-owner Michel Bras's masterful *cuisine du terroir*. Rte. de l'Aubrac, Laguiole; 33-5/65-51-18-20; dinner for two ●●●●●.

WHAT TO SEE & DO

Musée Fenaille The sizeable collection includes Neolithic-era stone statues and relics from the Hundred Years' War. 14 Place Raynaldy, Rodez; 33-5/65-73-84-30; musee-fenaille.com

WHERE TO SHOP

Forge de Laguiole Hand-crafted knives with handles in everything from boxwood to turquoise. Rte. de l'Aubrac; 33-5/65-48-43-34.

BRUSSELS, BELGIUM

WHERE TO STAY

Hotel Amigo Stylish, centrally located property, a quick stroll from the best antiques dealers. 1–3 Rue de l'Amigo, 32-2/547-4747; hotelamigo.com; doubles from $$$$$.

WHERE TO SHOP

Costermans Well-established antiques dealer specializing in 18th-century wares. 5 Place du Grand Sablon; 32-2/512-2133.
Michel Lambrecht Vintage items, plus clever new objects refashioned from old parts. 18 Rue Watteau; 32-2/502-2729.
Vincent Colet Exquisitely designed industrial pieces. 15 Rue de la Régence; 32-2/512-0488.

ANTWERP, BELGIUM

WHERE TO STAY

De Witte Lelie Three historic, adjoining canal houses with chic interiors. 16–18 Keizerstraat; 32-3/226-1966; dewittelelie.be; doubles from $$$.
Room National B&B owned by designers Violetta and Vera Pepa. 24 Nationalestraat; 32-3/226-0700; roomnational.com; doubles from $$.

WHERE TO EAT

Dôme The hottest dining ticket, thanks to its precise take on classic French cuisine. 2 Grote Hondstraat; 32-3/239-9003; dinner for two ●●●●.
Dôme sur Mer Casual seafood brasserie. 1 Arendstraat; 32-3/281-7433; dinner for two ●●●.
Fiskebar Popular white-tiled

KEY

LODGING

under $150 = $
$150–$299 = $$
$300–$699 = $$$
$700–$999 = $$$$
$1,000 + up = $$$$$

DINING

under $25 = ●
$25–$74 = ●●
$75–$149 = ●●●
$150–$299 = ●●●●
$300 + up = ●●●●●

Danish café. 12–13 Marnixplaats; 32-3/257-1357; dinner for two ●●●.

WHERE TO SHOP

Baby Beluga Flouncy dresses in a boudoir-esque boutique. 1 Volksstraat; 32-3/289-9060.

Elsa In-the-know shoe emporium, owned by a former Dries Van Noten designer. 147 Nationalestraat; 32-3/226-8454.

Violetta & Vera Pepa Perfectly tailored collections by two sisters. 24 Nationalestraat; 32-3/238-0021.

Wouters & Hendrix Intricate, handcrafted jewelry. 13 Lange Gasthuisstraat; 32-3/231-6242.

Yamamoto Massive store from designer Yohji Yamamoto. 32 Nationalestraat; 32-3/213-2178.

ILULISSAT, GREENLAND

WHERE TO STAY

Hotel Arctic 66 guest rooms and five igloos with views of Disko Bay; staff can arrange dog sledding and boating excursions, as well as tours to the glacier. 299/944-153; hotel-arctic.gl; doubles from $$$.

GRYTHYTTAN, SWEDEN

WHERE TO STAY

Grythyttan Inn Cluster of 22 buildings with Swedish country-style interiors. 2 Prästgatan; 46-591/63300; grythyttan.com; doubles from $$$.

Loka Brunn Famed mineral springs spa with comfortable accommodations. 46-591/63100; lokabrunn.com; doubles from $$$.

WHERE TO EAT

Bredsjö Ostcafé Hearty lunches, and cheese from the adjacent sheep farm. Bredsjö; 46-587/61020; lunch for two ●●.

Grythyttan Inn Menu features ingredients from the neighboring forest, plus a 7,000-bottle wine cellar. 2 Prästgatan; 46-591/63300; dinner for two ●●●●.

Kantinen Hyttblecket Lakeside restaurant in a futuristic-looking barn. Nordic House of Culinary Art, 2 Sörälgsvägen; 46-591/34060; dinner for two ●●.

WHAT TO SEE & DO

Formens Hus Design museum showcasing the Scandinavian greats. 7 Sikforsvägen; 46-591/64360; hellefors.se.

Grythyttan Vin Favorite local source for cloudberry wine. Grythyttan Livsmedelsby; 46-591/19111.

ÅLAND ARCHIPELAGO, FINLAND

WHERE TO STAY

Hotell Arkipelag Roomy, friendly harborside hotel with saunas, pools, and a nightclub. Strandgatan, Mariehamn, Aland; 358-18/24-020; hotellarkipelag.com; doubles from $$.

Hotell Brudhäll In a traditional wooden building on the edge of an isolated inlet. Karlby, Kökar; 358-18/55-955; brudhall.com; doubles from $$.

WHERE TO EAT

Indigo Restaurant & Bar Updated regional specialties, served in an old stone warehouse. Nygatan, Mariehamn, Åland; 358-18/16-550; dinner for two ●●●.

WHAT TO SEE & DO

Pommern Ship Museum Early-20th-century Scottish cargo ship in mint condition. West Harbor, Mariehamn; 358-18/53-1421; pommern.ax.

ROTTERDAM, THE NETHERLANDS

WHERE TO STAY

Hotel Bazar 27-room city-center inn with globally inspired interiors. 16 Witte de Withstraat; 31-10/206-5151; hotelbazar.nl; doubles from $.

WHERE TO EAT

Café Bazar Excellent North African and Middle Eastern cuisine. 16 Witte de Withstraat; 31-10/206-5151; dinner for two from ●●.

Euromast Brasserie menu, served 607 feet up in the sky. 20 Parkhaven; 31-10/241-1788; dinner for two ●●●.

Las Palmas Dutch star-chef Herman den Blijker's newest venture. 330 Wilhelminakade; 31-10/234-5122; dinner for two ●●●●.

WHAT TO SEE & DO

The Kunsthal Exhibits change constantly and range from Impressionism to lingerie. 341 Westzeedijk; 31-10/440-0301; kunsthal.nl.

Netherlands Architecture Institute Provides the ideal primer on Dutch architecture. 25 Museumpark; 31-10/440-1200; nai.nl.

TRANSPORT

Watertaxi Rotterdam The easiest and most scenic way to get around town. 31-10/403-0303; watertaxirotterdam.nl.

BERLIN

WHERE TO STAY

Adlon Kempinski Landmark hotel (rebuilt and reopened in 1997) with brocade-filled interiors. 77 Unter den Linden; 800/426-3135 or 49-30/2261-1016; hotel-adlon.de; doubles from $$$.

Hotel de Rome 19th-century landmark redone by the Rocco Forte group. 37 Behrenstrasse; 888/667-9477 or 49-30/460-6090; roccofortehotels.com; doubles from $$$.

WHAT TO SEE & DO

Altes Museum 1822 Neoclassical landmark with extensive antiquities collections. 1-3 Bodestrasse, Museuminsel; 49-30/2090-5555; smb.museum.

WHERE TO SHOP

Bonbonmacherei Sweets made from ancient recipes and with vintage equipment. 32 Oranienburger Strasse; 49-30/4405-5243.

ST. MORITZ, SWITZERLAND

WHERE TO STAY

Badrutt's Palace Hotel Extravagant grande-dame that is as of-the-moment as ever. 27 Via Serlas; 800/223-6800 or 41-81/837-1000; badruttspalace.com; doubles from $$$$.

Suvretta House The most traditional of St. Moritz's luxury hotels. 1 Via Chasellas; 41-81/836-3636; suvrettahouse.ch; doubles from $$$.

WHERE TO EAT

El Paradiso Mountainside dining in a post-and-beam room, or on the terrace overlooking the valley. Via Engiadina; 41-81/833-4002;

lunch for two ●●●.
La Marmite Over-the-top (waitresses wear ruffled Heidi-like aprons), but delicious. Corviglia; 41-81/833-6355; lunch for two ●●●●.

LANGHE, ITALY

WHERE TO STAY

L'Antico Asilo Charming and spotless family-run inn overlooking hillside vineyards. 13 Via Mazzini, Serralunga d'Alba; 39-0173/613-016; anticoasilo.com; doubles from $.
Villa Tiboldi A formerly underrated villa—until Paul Allen rented out the entire place during the 2006 Winter Olympics. 127 Case Sparse Tiboldi; 39-0173/970-388; villa tiboldi.it; doubles from $$.

WHERE TO EAT

La Ciau del Torravento. Ambitious and consistently excellent, with a stellar wine list. 7 Piazza Baracco, Treiso. 39-0173/638-333; dinner for two ●●●●.

WHAT TO SEE & DO

La Spinetta Wines that are decidedly new wave, but so well made that old-school purists love them too. 1 Via Carzello, Grinzane Cavour; 39-0141/877-396.
Pio Cesare Azienda Agricola To sample classic Piemontese wines. 6 Via Cesare Balbo, Alba; 39-0173/440-386.

EMILIA-ROMAGNA, ITALY

WHERE TO STAY

Grand Hotel Baglioni Luxe rooms and standout service, just off Bologna's main square. 8 Via Indipendenza; Bologna; 39-051/225-445; doubles from $$$.
Starhotels Excelsior Bright, contemporary rooms across from the Bologna train station. 51 Viale Pietramellara; Bologna; 39-051/246-178; starhotels.com; doubles from $$$.

WHAT TO SEE & DO

Arch of Augustus Built in 27 B.C. At the southeastern end of Corso d' Augusto, Rimini.
Basilica of San Domenico Site of the saint's tomb, carved by Nicola Pisano. 13 Piazza di San Domenico, Bologna.
Basilica of San Vitale Ornate sixth-century mosaics. Via San Vitale, Ravenna; 39-0544/219-518.
Ferrara Cathedral A 12th-century duomo with a pristine triple-arched façade. Piazza Cattedrale, Ferrara; 39-0532/207-449.
Galla Placidia Fifth-century mausoleum of Galla Placidia, who was captured by the Visigoths during the siege of Rome. Via San Vitale, Ravenna.
Palazzo dei Diamanti Dazzling palace designed by architect Biagio Rosetti in the late 15th century. 21 Corso Ercole d'Este, Ferrara; 39-0532/205-844.
Piazza Maggiore Bologna's central square. At the southern end of Via dell'Indipendenza.
Tempio Malatestiano Eccentric medieval church with a chapel clad in pagan astrological signs. 35 Via IV Novembre, Rimini.

PONZA, ITALY

WHERE TO STAY

Casa Vacanze Rosa Dei Venti Friendly beachfront boarding house. Via Spiaggia S. Maria; 39-0771/801-559; doubles from $.
Grand Hotel Chiaia di Luna Pastel-colored complex on a secluded cliff. Via Panoramica; 39-0771/801-113; hotel chiaiadiluna.com; doubles from $$$.
Villa Laetitia Anna Fendi Venturini's B&B, in a 1920's house. Via Scotti; 39-0771/809-886; villa laetitia.it; doubles from $$$.

WHERE TO EAT

Ristorante Il Tramonto Delectable antipasti, and unobstructed views of the uninhabited island of Palmarola. Campo Inglese, Le Forna; 39-0771/808-563; dinner for two ●●●.

SICILY, ITALY

WHERE TO STAY

Caol Ishka A chic inn on the grounds of a former farm. Via Elorina, Contrada Pantanelli, Siracusa; 39-0931/69057; caolishka.com; doubles from $$$.
Casa Talía Urbane B&B occupying five adjacent houses. 1/9 Via Exaudinos, Modica; 39-0932/752-075; casatalia.it; doubles from $$.

WHERE TO EAT

Antica Dolceria Bonajuto Famous for its stuffed *impanatiggi*. 159 Corso Umberto I, Modica; 39-0932/941-225.
Caffè Sicilia Perhaps the best sweets on the island. 125 Corso Vittorio Emanuele, Noto; 39-0931/835-013.
Masseria degli Ulivi Contemporary versions of traditional dishes. Contrada Porcari, Noto; 39-0931/813-019; lunch for two ●.
Restaurante Duomo The region's only Michelin two-star establishment. 31 Via Capitano Bocchieri, Ragusa; 39-0932/651-265; dinner for two ●●●.
Zafferano Bistrot Inventive cooking from part-Sicilian-part-Kenyan chef Massimo Giaquinta. Via Elorina, Contrada Pantanelli, Siracusa; 39-0931/69057; dinner for two ●●●.

WHAT TO SEE & DO

COS Winery Earthy, elemental wines (such as the 2003 Cerasuolo) from an iconoclastic producer. S.P. 3 Acate, Chiaremonte Ragusa; 39-0932/876-145.

KÍTHIRA, GREECE

WHERE TO STAY

Hotel Margarita 12-room manse with a pretty patio. Hora; 30-273/603-1711; hotel-margarita.com; doubles from $$.
Pitsinades Six-room guest house built around courtyards. Aroniádika; 30-273/603-3877; pitsinades.com; doubles from $.

WHERE TO EAT

Zorba's Greek specialities, fresh from the grill. Hora; 30-273/603-1655; dinner for two ●●.

KEY

LODGING

under $150 = $
$150–$299 = $$
$300–$699 = $$$
$700–$999 = $$$$
$1,000 + up = $$$$$

DINING

under $25 = ●
$25–$74 = ●●
$75–$149 = ●●●
$150–$299 = ●●●●
$300 + up = ●●●●●

EASTERN EUROPE

MARIENBAD, CZECH REPUBLIC

WHERE TO STAY

Grandhotel Pupp Stately property in its fourth century of business. 2 Mírové námestí, Karlsbad; 420-353/109-111; pupp.cz; doubles from $$$.

Hotel Nové Lázně Grande-dame that still houses what was Edward VII's favorite mineral bath. 53 Reitenbergerova, Marienbad; 420-354/644-111; marienbad.cz; doubles from $$, including meals and spa.

MONTENEGRO

WHERE TO STAY

Bianca Resort & Spa Striking contemporary lodge deep in the forest. 81210 Mirka Vesovica, Kolasin; 382-81/863-000; biancaresort.com; doubles from $$.

Planinka Hotel Ski-town accommodations with blond-wood interiors. Žabljak, Durmitor National Park; 382-89/361-344; doubles from $.

SARAJEVO

WHERE TO STAY

Halvat Guest House Family-run B&B in the city's atmospheric Old Town. 5 Kasima Efendije Dobrae; 387-33/237-714; halvat.com.ba; doubles from $.

Holiday Inn Sarajevo Bright-yellow, longtime headquarters for foreign journalists; it's still good value. 4 Zmaja Od Bosne; 888/465-4329 or 387-33/288-000; holiday-inn.com; doubles from $$.

Villa Orient Welcoming, centrally located hotel. 6 Oprkanj; 387-33/232-702; hotel-villa-orient.com; doubles from $$.

DANUBE DELTA, ROMANIA

WHERE TO STAY & WHAT TO DO

Delta Nature Resort 30 eco-friendly villas, plus a staff that organizes excursions to area attractions. Somova-Parches, Km 3, Tulcea; 40-21/311-4532; deltaresort.com; doubles from $$$, including transfers from Bucharest.

KIEV, UKRAINE

WHERE TO STAY

Hyatt Regency Comfortable hotel with a state-of-the-art fitness center. 5A Alla Tarasova Ul.; 888/591-1234 or 380-44/581-1234; hyatt.com; doubles from $$$$.

Radisson SAS Hotel Landmark building within walking distance of many sites. 2 Yaroslaviv Val; 888/333-3333 or 380-44/492-2200; radissonsas.com; doubles from $$$.

WHERE TO EAT

Belvedere Frequented by boldface locals. 1 Dneprovsky Spusk; 380-44/288-5070; dinner for two ●●●●.

Ikra Seafood and oyster bar. 11 Pankovskaya Ul.; 380-44/288-1990; dinner for two ●●●●.

WHAT TO SEE & DO

Pinchuk Art Centre Outstanding collection of contemporary art. 1/3-2A. Krasnoarmeyskaya-Basseynaya Ul.; 380-44/590-0858; pinchukart centre.org.

WHERE TO SHOP

Passazh Complex High-end Russian and Ukrainian boutiques. 15 Khreschatik Ul.

NIGHTLIFE

Babuin Cabaret-style bookstore, café, and bar. 39 Bogdana Khmelnytskogo Ul.; 380-44/234-1503.

Decadence House The city's top late-night spot. 16 Shota Rustaveli Ul.; 380-44/206-4920.

MOSCOW

WHERE TO STAY

Golden Apple 92-room, high-design hotel. 11 Malaya Dmitrovka Ul.; 7-495/980-7000; golden apple.ru; doubles from $$$.

Hotel Baltschug Kempinski Old World pampering, and views of Red Square. 1 Balchug Ul.; 800/426-3135 or 7-495/287-2000; kempinski-moscow.com; doubles from $$$$.

Ritz-Carlton The city's flashiest new digs. 3 Tverskaya Ul.; 800/241-3333 or 7-495/225-8888; ritzcarlton.com; doubles from $$$$.

WHERE TO EAT

Café Pushkin Round-the-clock caviar. 26A Tverskoy Bul.; 7-495/739-0033; dinner for two ●●●●.

The Most French-influenced cuisine in czar-ready surroundings. 6/3 Kuznetsky Most; 7-495/660-0706; dinner for two ●●●●.

WHAT TO SEE & DO

Art 4 Talk-of-the-town contemporary art museum. 4 Hlinovsky Tupik; 7-495/660-1158; art4.ru.

New Tretyakov Gallery 20th-century Russian masters. 10 Krymsky Val; 7-495/238-1378.

WHERE TO SHOP

Tsum For sharp, street-wise clothes. 2 Petrovka Ul.; 7-495/933-7300.

ISTANBUL

WHERE TO STAY

Ansen Suites Up-to-the-minute interiors behind a centuries-old façade. 130 Mesrutiyet Cad.; 90-212/245-8808; ansensuites.com; doubles from $$$.

Misafir Suites In the heart of Beyoğlu. 1 Gazeteci Erol Dernek Sk.; 90-212/249-8930; misafirsuites.com; doubles from $$$.

WHERE TO EAT

Mikla Istanbul's most confident modern restaurant. 167–185 Mesrutiyet Cad.; 90-212/293-5656; dinner for two ●.

WHERE TO SHOP

Alaturca Top antiques store, in a historic house. 4 Faikpasa Sk.; 90-212/245-2933.

Haci Bekir Have made Turkish delight since 1777. 129 Istiklal Cad.; 90-212/245-2933.

NIGHTLIFE

Babylon Intimate live-music club. 3 Sehbender Sk.; 90-212/292-7368.

Nu Pera Dancing hot-spot. 149–6 Mesrutiyet Cad.; 90-212/245-6070.

Refik Beloved traditional drinking house. 10–12 Sofyali Sk.; 90-212/243-2834.

Yakup 2 A cavernous pub. 35–37 Asmali Mescit Cad.; 90-212/249-2925.

KEY

LODGING

under $150 = $
$150–$299 = $$
$300–$699 = $$$
$700–$999 = $$$$
$1,000 + up = $$$$$

DINING

under $25 = ●
$25–$74 = ●●
$75–$149 = ●●●
$150–$299 = ●●●●
$300 + up = ●●●●●

AFRICA + THE MIDDLE EAST

ADDIS ABABA, ETHIOPIA

WHERE TO STAY

Hilton Addis Ababa 10-floor tower with manicured grounds. Menelik II Ave.; 800/445-8667 or 251-115/518-400; hilton.com; doubles from $$.

Sheraton Addis Hotel of choice for UN staffers. Taitu St.; 800/325-3589 or 251-115/171-717; starwoodhotels.com; doubles from $$$.

WHERE TO EAT & DRINK

Gonder Tej Bet Delicious honey wine made on the premises. In the *merkato*; dinner for two ●.

Habesha Top spot for authentic Ethiopian food, with a pleasant patio. Bole Rd.; 251-115/518-358; dinner for two ●.

MADAGASCAR

WHERE TO STAY

Anjajavy L'Hôtel The country's most luxurious option: rosewood villas on a nature-reserve peninsula. Menabe Sakalava; 33-1/44-69-15-03; anjajavy.com; doubles from $$$$$, three-night minimum.

Le Domaine de Fontenay Colonial country-house hotel. Joffreville Antsiranana 2; 261-33/113-4581; lefontenay-madagascar.com; doubles from $$.

Vakôna Forest Lodge Thatched-roof lakeside bungalows surrounded by forest. Near Andasibe; 261-20/222-1394; hotel-vakona.com; doubles from $.

MADIKWE PRIVATE GAME RESERVE, SOUTH AFRICA

WHERE TO STAY

Madikwe Safari Lodge 16 suites with private plunge pools, in one of Africa's largest wildlife parks. 888/882-3742; ccafrica.com; doubles from $$$$, including meals and game drives.

THE KAROO, SOUTH AFRICA

WHERE TO STAY

Boesmanskop Two-room inn filled with Cape Dutch antiques. R62, Oudtshoorn; 27-44/213-3365; boesmanskop.co.za; doubles from $, including dinner.

De Bergkant Lodge Stylish guesthouse in a historic village. 5 Church St., Prince Albert; 27-23/541-1088; dewaterkant.co.za; doubles from $$.

Feather Palace A pair of cottages on a working ostrich farm. Guest Farm R62, Oudtshoorn; 27-44/251-6760; thefeatherpalace.co.za; doubles from $.

WHERE TO EAT

Ronnies Sex Shop Roadside bar and burger joint. R62, 16 miles east of Barrydale; 27-28/572-1153; lunch for two ●.

WHAT TO SEE & DO

Bergwater Vineyards The Karoo's first winery. Prince Albert Valley; 27-23/541-1703.

Swartriver Olive Farm Tour the groves, then taste their bounty. R353; 27-23/541-1917; by appointment.

SWARTLAND, SOUTH AFRICA

WHERE TO STAY

Bartholomeus Klip Farmhouse Tranquil four-room inn on a sprawling farm. Bo Hermon Rd., R44, Hermon; 27-22/448-1820; bartholomeusklip.com; doubles from $$$, including dinner and a game drive.

Royal Hotel 146-year-old manor house, fresh from an extensive renovation. 33 Main St., Riebeek Kasteel; 27-22/448-1378; royalinriebeek.com; doubles from $$.

WHAT TO SEE & DO

Allesverloren Wine Estate Vineyard that's been family-owned for five generations. Rte. 311, Riebeek West; 27-22/461-2320.

Kloovenburg Limited-edition Cabernet Sauvignon and Cabernet-based blends, plus house-made jams, pestos, and chutneys. R46, Riebeek Kasteel; 27-22/448-1635.

Pulpit Rock Forward-thinking winery, with a tasting-room that sells regional snacks such as *droewörs* (local-game sausages). Rte. 311, near Riebeek West; 27-22/461-2025.

Sadie Family Estate Innovative producer making wines inspired by traditional methods. Aprilskloof Rd., Paardeberg; 27-21/482-3138.

TUNIS, TUNISIA

WHERE TO STAY

Dar El Medina A private mansion turned hotel in the city's ancient quarter. 64 Rue Sidi Ben Arous; 216-71/563-022; darelmedina.com; doubles from $$.

WHERE TO EAT

Dar El Jeld Excellent Tunisian food in a converted medina palace. 5-10 Rue Dar el Jeld; 216-71/560-916; dinner for two ●●●.

WHAT TO SEE & DO

Bardo National Museum One of the world's best collections of Roman mosaics. 216-71/513-650.

DOHA, QATAR

WHERE TO STAY

Four Seasons Hotel Centrally located towers surrounding a private beach. The Corniche; 800/332-3442 or 011-974/494-8888; fourseasons.com; doubles from $$$.

Ritz-Carlton Classic opulence on the Arabian Gulf. West Bay Lagoon; 800/241-3333 or 011-974/484-8000; ritzcarlton.com; doubles from $$$.

Ritz-Carlton Sharq Village & Spa Low-rise complex modeled after a Qatari village. Ras Abu Aboud St.; 800/241-3333 or 011-974/425-6666; ritzcarlton.com; doubles from $$$.

WHAT TO SEE & DO

Museum of Islamic Art An extensive collection spanning more than 1,000 years, in a stunning, just-opened I. M. Pei-designed building. The Corniche.

KEY

LODGING

under $150 = $
$150–$299 = $$
$300–$699 = $$$
$700–$999 = $$$$
$1,000 + up = $$$$$

DINING

under $25 = ●
$25–$74 = ●●
$75–$149 = ●●●
$150–$299 = ●●●●
$300 + up = ●●●●●

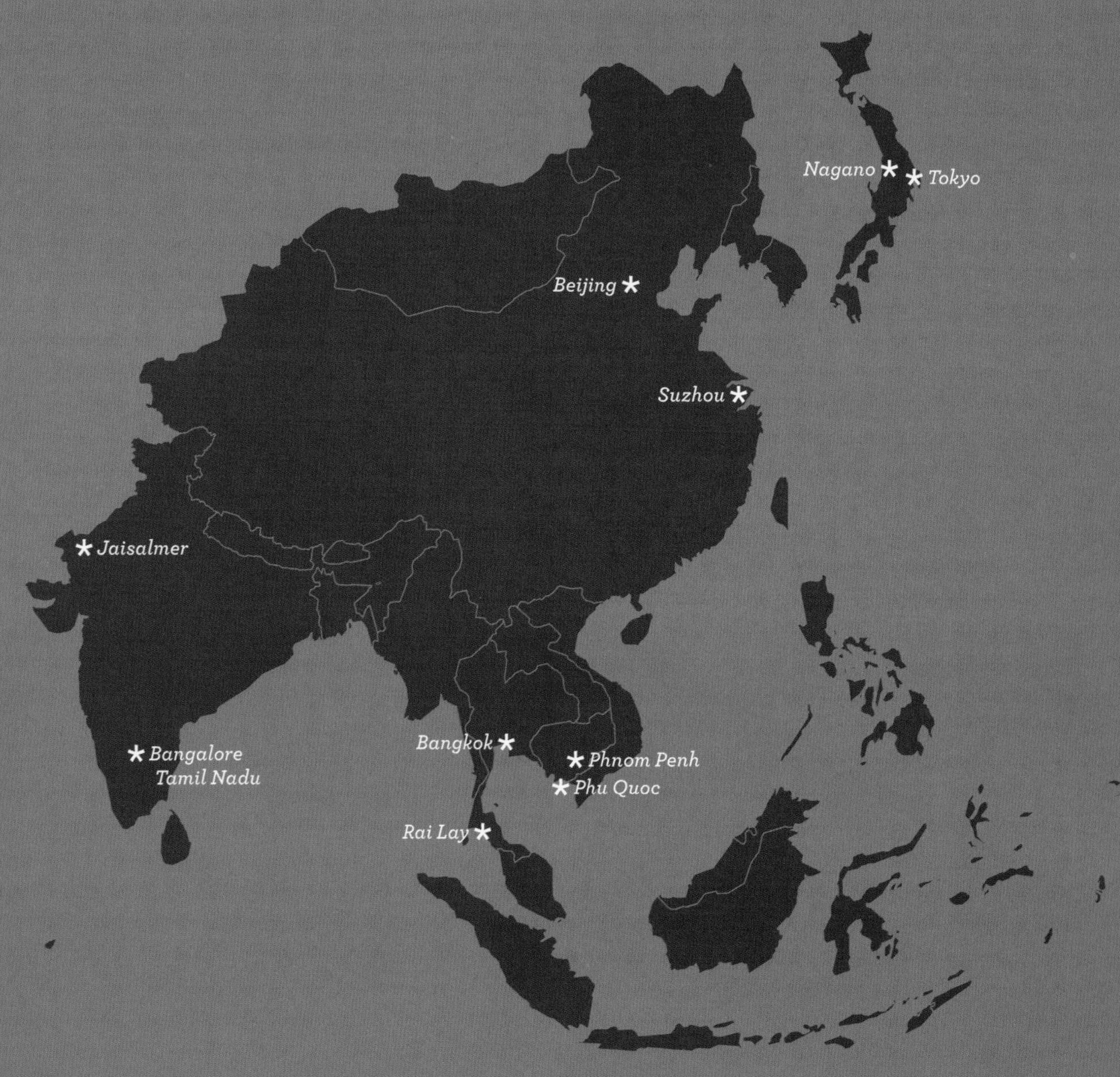
Nagano
Tokyo
Beijing
Suzhou
Jaisalmer
Bangalore
Tamil Nadu
Bangkok
Phnom Penh
Phu Quoc
Rai Lay

ASIA

TOKYO

WHERE TO STAY

Park Hyatt Iconic hotel occupying the top 14 floors of a striking 52-story Kenzo Tange-designed tower. 3-7-1-2 Nishi Shinjuku, Shinjuku-ku; 800/233-1234 or 81-3/5322-1234; hyatt.com; doubles from $$$.

Peninsula Tokyo Glam new hotel near the Ginza shopping district, with spacious guest rooms and four subway lines in the basement. 1-8-1 Yurakucho, Chiyoda-ku; 866/382-8388 or 81-3/6270-2888; peninsula.com; doubles from $$$.

WHERE TO SHOP

Chanel Ginza Housed in a daring Peter Marino-designed black-and-white cube. 3-5-3 Ginza, Chuo-ku; 81-3/5159-5555.

Issey Miyake The conceptual, iconoclastic designer's flagship store; the window displays alone are worth a visit. 3-18-11 Minami-Aoyama, Minato-ku; 81-3/3423-1408.

Laforet Harajuku The city's trend factory: dozens of shops specializing in what's newest for the younger set, all under one roof. 1-11-6 Jingumae, Shibuya-ku; 81-3/3475-0411.

Louis Vuitton The building's innovative façade incorporates 30,000 stacked glass tubes. 5-7-5 Jingumae, Shibuya-ku; 81-3/3478-2100.

Metamorphose Harajuku Headquarters for the wildly popular cutie-pie Lolita look. Scenic Sekine Building, 6-28-4 Jingumae, Shibuya-ku; 81-3/3406-6978.

Mikimoto Long-established pearl purveyor in a dazzling new space. 2-4-12 Ginza, Chuo-ku; 81-3/3562-3130.

Omotesando Hills Mall with every imaginable high-end shop, from the predictable to the unexpected. 4-12-10 Jingumae, Shibuya-ku; 81-3/3497-0310.

Tabio Socks and tights in a dazzling array of colors and patterns (they make great souvenirs). In Omestesdando Hills, 4-12-10 Jingumae, Shibuya-ku; 81-3/5785- 0561.

UES Small shop stocking cross-cultural staples like plaid lumberjack jackets, flannel shirts, and a full range of Japanese denim. Apiadaikanama 101, 26-7 Sarugaku-cho, Shibuya-ku; 81-3/3462-7471.

Undercover Revered temple of sartorial excess, with elegantly made yet notoriously strange clothing. 5-3-18 Unimat Bleu Cinq Point C-1F, Minamiaoyama, Minato-ku; 81-3/3407-1232.

Wako Beautiful old-world department store that features an elegant curved staircase and superb if quiet merchandise. 4-5-11 Ginza, Chuo-ku; 81-3/3562-2111.

Yohji Yamamoto The flagship store's avante-garde look matches the designer's adventurous spirit. 5-3-6 Minami-Aoyama, Minato-ku; 81-3/3409-6006.

NAGANO, JAPAN

WHERE TO STAY

The Hanaya 300-year-old *ryokan* that has been in the same family for nine generations. Tsumagoshuku, Nagisomachi, Kiso-gun; 81-26/457-3106; doubles from $, including meals.

Oyado Kinenkan Three-story *ryokan* on a quiet backstreet lined with mom-and-pop stores; they have been accepting guests for more than a hundred years. 550 Nishi-machi; 81-26/234-2043; doubles from $, including meals.

WHERE TO EAT

Zawacc Caffé Bright, airy coffee house overlooking the Zenko-ji temple. 486 Motoyoshi Cho; 81-26/232-3359.

WHAT TO SEE & DO

M-Wave Two high-tech skating rinks, plus a museum with artifacts from the 1998 Winter Olympic Games, which were held in the city. 81-26/222-3300.

Zenko-ji Seventh-century Buddhist temple that has long been a magnet for travelers; a prayer chamber is open to visitors. Motoyoshi Cho 491; 81-26/234-3591.

BEIJING

WHERE TO STAY

Hotel Kapok A partially transparent exterior meant to mimic a lantern, and clean, basic rooms. 16 Donghuamen St.; 86-10/6525-9988; hotelkapok.com; doubles from $.

Peninsula Beijing Lavish interiors inspired by traditional Chinese motifs, within walking distance of the Forbidden City and Tiananmen Square. 8 Goldfish Lane, Wangfujing; 800/223-6800 or 86-10/8516-2888; peninsula.com; doubles from $$$.

St. Regis Opulent hotel fresh from an extensive renovation; the dramatic glass-enclosed pool has city views. 21 Jianguomen Wai Dajie; 877/787-3447 or 86-10/6460-6688; starwoodhotels.com; doubles from $$$.

WHAT TO SEE & DO

2008 Olympic Park Herzog & de Meuron's stadium is a streamlined tangle of metal that redefines the city's skyline. 267 Fourth

---

KEY

LODGING

- under $150 = **$**
- $150–$299 = **$$**
- $300–$699 = **$$$**
- $700–$999 = **$$$$**
- $1,000 + up = **$$$$$**

DINING

- under $25 = ●
- $25–$74 = ●●
- $75–$149 = ●●●
- $150–$299 = ●●●●
- $300 + up = ●●●●●

Ring Rd.; 86-10/6669-9185; beijing2008.com.

China Central Television Headquarters Gargantuan, contorted arch (the second-largest building in the world) designed by avant-gardists Rem Koolhaas and Ole Scheeren. Central Business District; cctv.com.

Forbidden City A ceremonial center since 1420, impeccably restored in 2008 in an unprecedented international effort. 86-10/6513-2255; dpm.org.cn.

National Grand Theater Paul Andreu's bold titanium-and-glass bubble rises from a reflecting pool in the middle of the city. 4 Shi Beihutong; 86-10/6606-4705; nationalgrandtheater.com.

Planning Exhibition Hall Devoted to installations and shows that document the city's growth. 20 E. Qianmen Ave., Chóngwén; 86-10/6702-4559.

Summer Palace China's largest imperial garden, now a UNESCO World Heritage site. 19 Xinjian Gongmen, Haidan; 86-10/6288-1144.

Temple of Heaven Taoist complex with a gabled, circular prayer space (the Hall for Good Harvests). Tiantan Donglu; 86-10/6702-8866.

SUZHOU, CHINA

WHERE TO STAY

Renaissance Suzhou Hotel Centrally located property, overlooking a park. 229 Su Hua Rd; 800/468-3571 or 86-51/2676-18888; marriott.com, doubles from $.

Sheraton Suzhou Hotel & Towers Sprawling luxury complex with design details influenced by traditional Chinese architecture. 259 Xinshi Rd.; 800/325-3535 or 86-51/6510-3388; starwoodhotels.com; doubles from $$.

WHAT TO SEE & DO

Garden for Lingering In Six-acre UNESCO World Heritage site that is more than 400 years old, and is one of the best loved and most well-known gardens in China. Next to Changmen Gate.

Suzhou Museum More than 30,000 items—including important collections of Ming and Qing Dynasty paintings and calligraphy—showcased in a stunning new I.M. Pei-designed building. 204 Dong Bei St.; 86-512/6757-5666; szmuseum.com.

TAMIL NADU, INDIA

WHERE TO STAY

The Bangala 13-room hotel in a former men's club; excellent service. 1 Senjai Oorani South St., Karaikudi; 91-45/6522-0221; the bangala.com; doubles from $.

Taj Coromandel Wood-paneled interiors decorated with brightly colored textiles in a city-center high-rise. 37 Mahatma Gandhi Rd., Nungambakkam, Chennai; 866/969-1825 or 91-44/6600-2827; tajhotels.com; doubles from $$$.

Taj Garden Retreat Tranquil lakeside property on a converted 123-year-old colonial bungalow estate. Pasumalai, Madurai; 866/969-1825 or 91-45/2237-1601; tajhotels.com; doubles from $$.

WHAT TO SEE & DO

Chennai Government Museum Impressive collection of ancient sculptures, including famous bronzes of the multi-armed Shiva. 486 Pantheon Rd., Egmore, Chennai; 91-44/2819-3238; chennai museum.org.

Chettinad Museum Artifacts documenting local history, housed in a classic Chettiar mansion (marble floors, teak columns, tiled roofs). Kanadukathan, Chettinad.

Meenakshi Sundareswara Temple Exuberant, sculpture-covered 16th-century landmark. Madurai; 91-452/234-4360.

Thanjavur Royal Palace and Museums One of the world's most important libraries of palm-leaf manuscripts. Thanjavur.

BANGALORE, INDIA

WHERE TO STAY

Leela Palace Opulent 9-acre spread surrounded by gardens. 23 Airport Rd.; 91-80/521-1234; theleela.com; doubles from $$.

Park Bangalore Terence Conran-designed property in the center of town; the lounge, I-Bar, is a popular watering hole. 14/7 Mahatma Gandhi Rd.; 91-80/2559-4666; theparkhotels.com; doubles from $$$.

JAISALMER, INDIA

WHERE TO STAY

Deepak Rest House Family-run hostelry with basic rooms and a pleasant rooftop restaurant. Behind the Jain temple complex; 91-2992/252-665; doubles from $.

Gorbandh Palace Former residence of a maharajah; the staff can organize excursions into the desert. No. 1 Tourist Complex, Sam Rd.; 91-2992/253-801; hrh hotels.com; doubles from $$.

Hotel Killa Bhawan Two converted townhouses (built directly into the fort's sandstone walls), decorated with traditional Rajasthani furniture and vividly hued silks. 445 Kotri Para; 91-2992/251-204; killabhawan.com; doubles from $$.

WHAT TO SEE & DO

Jain Temples Series of extraordinary prayer sites, constructed between the 14th and 16th centuries and linked by passageways; the elaborate relief carvings depict the religion's prophets.

BANGKOK

WHERE TO STAY

Millennium Hilton Tower hotel on the west bank of the Chao Phraya, with great river views and a roof-top infinity pool. 123 Charoen Nakorn Rd., Klongsan; 800/445-

8667 or 66-2/442-2000; hilton.com; doubles from $$.

The Oriental Legendary 1887 hotel and modern tower on the river, with teak furnishings and Thai textiles. 48 Oriental Ave.; 800/526-6566 or 66-2/659-9000; mandarinoriental.com; doubles from $$$.

Peninsula Bangkok 37-story hotel that's among the city's most luxe, on the Chao Phraya. 333 Charoen Nakorn Rd.; 866/382-8388 or 66-2/861-2888; peninsula.com; doubles from $$$

Shangri-La Expansive two-tower riverfront complex with tropical gardens. 89 Soi Wat Suan Plu New Rd.; 866/565-5050 or 66-2/236-7777; shangri-la.com; doubles from $$$.

WHERE TO EAT

The Verandah The Oriental's informal spot for breakfast, lunch, and dinner, with landscaped gardens and a serene terrace fronting the river. 48 Oriental Ave.; 66-2/659-9000; dinner for two ●●●.

TOUR OPERATOR

Manohra Cruises Multi-night river excursions aboard lavishly converted antique rice barges. 66-2/477-0770; manohracruises.com; three-night cruise for two from $$$$$, including meals.

RAI LAY, THAILAND

WHERE TO STAY

Railei Beach Club Cluster of privately owned houses, available for rent and inspired by traditional Thai architecture. 66/866-859-359; raileibeachclub.com; houses from $.

The Rayavadee 98 airy two-story pavilions (some with private pools) and four villas—set in the jungle or overlooking Phranang Beach. 66-75/620-7403; rayavadee.com; doubles from $$$$.

Sand Sea Simple bungalows on the west beach. 66-75/622-574; sandsearesort.com; doubles from $.

WHERE TO EAT

The Grotto Tucked against a limestone cliff, right on the beach; grilled dishes include chicken skewers and pineapple chunks. At the Rayavadee; dinner for two ●●.

Krua Phranang Thai specialties such as *yum talay* (spicy seafood salad) and *chu chi goong* (prawns in red curry). At the Rayavadee; 66-75/620-7403; dinner for two ●●●.

WHAT TO SEE & DO

King Climbers Guided cliff-climbing for all skill levels. Main office is located in the Ya Ya Bungalows, East Rai Lay Beach; railay.com.

PHNOM PENH, CAMBODIA

WHERE TO STAY

Amanjaya Pancam Hotel Intimate all-suite property on the Mekong, with rosewood floors, Buddhist statues, and silk tapestries. 1, Sisowath Quay, Corner St. 154; 855-23/214-747; amanjaya.com; doubles from $$.

The Pavilion 18-room hotel in an elegant 1920's house, across from the Wat Botum pagoda. 27, St. 19, Khan Daun Penh; 855-23/222-280; pavilion-cambodia.com; doubles from $.

Raffles Hotel Le Royal Restored 1929 French-colonial mansion with lush gardens, in the center of town. 92 Rukhak Vithei Daun Penh, off Monivong Blvd.; 855-23/981-888; raffles.com; doubles from $$$.

WHAT TO SEE & DO

National Museum A trove of Khmer artifacts from the 4th through the 13th centuries. Corner of Sts. 178 and 13; 855-23/211-753.

Royal Palace Three-compound complex that houses, among other things, an impressive collection of Buddha statues (carved from crystal; encrusted with diamonds). Samdech Sothearos Blvd., between Sts. 184 and 240.

Russian Market For anything from fine ceramic dishes to frogs' legs; excellent souvenir hunting. Corner of Sts. 163 and 444, south of Mao Tse Toung Blvd.

Tuol Sleng Genocide Museum Weapons, photographs, and other sobering items from the reign of the Khmer Rouge, located in a former prisoner detention center. Corner of Sts. 113 and 350; 855-23/216-045.

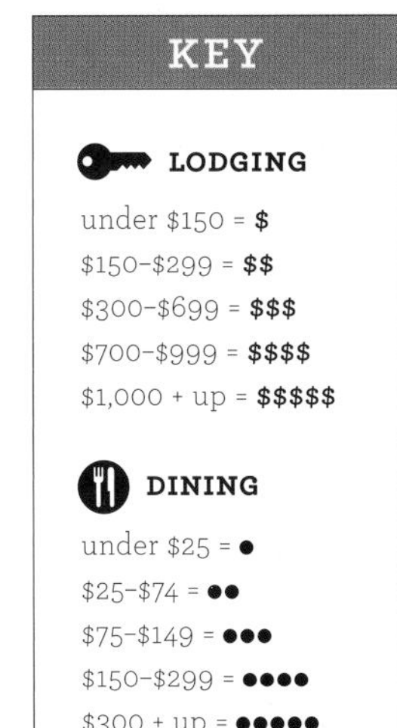

PHU QUOC, VIETNAM

WHERE TO STAY

Grand Mercure La Veranda Resort & Spa 43-room oceanfront retreat that recalls a colonial plantation, down to the paddle fans and tropical gardens. Tran Hung Dao St., Bai Truong; 800/221-4542 or 84-77/398-2988; laverandaresort.com; doubles from $$.

WHERE TO EAT

Gio Bien Friendly joint with hammocks and tables under causarina trees, and possibly the best grilled squid you'll ever taste. On the beach at Mui Duong, Ganh Dau District; 84-77/384-5507; lunch for two ●.

Palm Tree Homey family-run beach shack open from dawn until late at night, serving grilled seafood and chilled fresh coconuts. Bai Truong, next door to La Veranda; lunch for two ●.

AUSTRALIA + NEW ZEALAND + THE SOUTH PACIFIC

SYDNEY

WHERE TO STAY

The Establishment Chic 33-room hotel with monochromatic interiors, in the CBD. 5 Bridge Lane; 61-2/9240-3100; luxehotels.com; doubles from $$$.

Park Hyatt Art-filled waterfront low-rise with Opera House views. 7 Hickson Rd.; 800/233-1234 or 61-2/9241-1234; park.hyatt.com; doubles from $$$$.

WHERE TO EAT

Billy Kwong Sophisticated Chinese food, served in a slender shopfront. 355 Crown St., Shop 3, Surry Hills; 61-2/9332-3300; dinner for two ●●●.

Chinese Noodle Restaurant Specializes in the hearty dishes of northern China. 8 Quay St. (enter on Thomas St.), Chinatown; 61-2/9281-9051; dinner for two ●●.

Ichi-ban Boshi Popular ramen joint. Galeries Victoria, Level 2, 500 George St., Town Hall; 61-2/9262-7677; dinner for two ●.

The Malaya A Sydney institution, with spot-on Malaysian food. 39 Lime St., King St. Wharf, Darling Harbour; 61-2/9279-1170; dinner for two ●●.

Marigold Citymark For fantastic dim-sum. 683–689 George St., Levels 4 and 5, Chinatown; 61-2/9281-3388; dinner for two ●●●.

Spice I Am Tiny 20-seater that has the best Thai cooking in town. 90 Wentworth Ave., Surry Hills; 61-2/9280-0928; dinner for two ●●.

Tai Wong A no-frills, stand-out barbecue shop. 12 Campbell St., Chinatown; 61-2/9212-1481; dinner for two ●●.

Thanh Binh Fresh, vibrant Vietnamese food. 52 John St., Cabramatta; 61-2/9727-9729; dinner for two ●●●.

Yoshii Inventive Japanese. 115 Harrington St., The Rocks; 61-2/9247-2566; dinner for two ●●●●.

GREAT ALPINE ROAD, AUSTRALIA

WHERE TO STAY

Buckland Studio Retreat Four austere but posh cabins in the bush. McCormack's Lane, Buckland Valley; 61-3/5756-2383; thebuckland.com.au; studios from $$$ per night.

The Huski Mountainside apartment hotel. Stizmark St., Falls Creek; 61-1300/652-260; huski.com.au; doubles from $$$$$, two-night minimum.

WHERE TO EAT

Blue Duck Inn Down-home local favorites: vegetable pasties, fried trout. Omeo Hwy., Anglers Rest; 61-3/5159-7220; lunch for two ●●.

Crackenback Farm & Cottage Linen-covered tables, great sandwishes, perfect lemonade. Alpine Way, Thredbo Valley; 61-2/6456-2601; lunch for two ●●.

Simone's Much-lauded eatery preparing straightforward food with local ingredients. 98 Gavan St., Bright; 61-3/5755-2266; dinner for two ●●.

TASMANIA, AUSTRALIA

WHERE TO STAY

Hatherley House Stylish nine-room B&B. 43 High St.; Launceston; 61-3/6334-7727; hatherleyhouse.com.au; doubles from $$.

WHERE TO EAT

Daniel Alps at Strathlynn Ever-changing menu that features the freshest local produce. 95 Rosevears Dr., Rosevears; 61-3/6330-2388; lunch for two ●●●.

Lebrina Bistro that was at the vanguard of Tasmania's thriving food scene; as popular as ever. 155 New Town Rd., New Town, Hobart; 61-3/6228-7775; dinner for two ●●●●.

Peppermint Bay One of the best spots to sample the island's current food philosophy. 3435 Channel Hwy, Woodbridge; 61-3/6267-4088; dinner for two ●●●.

WHAT TO SEE & DO

Apsley Gorge Winery that produces outstanding Pinot Noirs. Rosedale Rd., Bicheno; 61-3/6375-1221.

Eureka Farm Superlative berries, chutneys, and jams. 89 Upper Scamander Rd., Scamander; 61-3/6372-5500.

Frogmore Creek For award-winning estate-bottled wines. 208 Denholms Rd., Penna; 61-3/6248-5844.

Moorilla Leading small-batch winery since 1958. 655 Main Rd., Berriedale; 61-3/6277-9900.

SOUTH ISLAND, NEW ZEALAND

WHERE TO STAY

Lake Brunner Lodge Updated 1930's lodge surrounded by protected forest. Kumara, Westland; 64-3/738-0163; lakebrunner.co.nz; doubles from $$$.

Rough & Tumble Bush Lodge Rustic rooms with rainforest views. Mokihinui Rd., Seddonville; 64-3/782-1337; roughandtumble.co.nz; doubles from $$$ including meals.

WHERE TO EAT

Bay House The west coast's finest chowder. Tauranga Bay, Cape Foulwind; 64-3/789-7133, dinner for two ●●●.

KEY

LODGING

under $150 = $
$150–$299 = $$
$300–$699 = $$$
$700–$999 = $$$$
$1,000 + up = $$$$$

DINING

under $25 = ●
$25–$74 = ●●
$75–$149 = ●●●
$150–$299 = ●●●●
$300 + up = ●●●●●

WANAKA, NEW ZEALAND

WHERE TO STAY

Whare Kea Lodge Six-room lakeside retreat; a mountain chalet is accessible only via helicopter. Mount Aspiring Rd.; 64-3/443-1400; wharekealodge.com; doubles from $$$$$.

WHERE TO EAT

Cardrona Hotel Excellent pub grub. Crown Range Rd., Cardrona; 64-3/443-8153; dinner for two ●●.

SOCIETY ISLANDS

WHERE TO STAY

Bora Bora Lagoon Resort & Spa Dreamy overwater digs. Bora-Bora; 800/860-4905 or 689/60-4000; doubles from $$$.

St. Regis Resort Polynesia at its most luxe. Bora-Bora; 800/598-1863 or 689/607-888; stregis.com; doubles from $$$$$.

Villa Corallina Colonial-style cottages. Moorea; 689/770-590; villacorallina.com; doubles from $$.

WHERE TO EAT

La Plage Spicy curries on a private islet. Motu Moea, Moorea; 689/749-696; lunch for two ●●●.

INDEX

INDEX

TRIPS DIRECTORY

CONTRIBUTORS

Richard Alleman
Tom Austin
Luke Barr
Andrea Bennet
Alan Brown
Joan Juliet Buck
Ian Buruma
Paul Chai
Marcelle Clements
Anthony Dennis
Bill Donahue
Simon Doonan
Charlotte Druckman
Amy Farley
Gayle Forman
Brett Forrest
Eleni N. Gage
Elizabeth Gilbert
Alison Goran
Jaime Gross
Darrell Hartman
Karrie Jacobs
David Kaufman
David A. Keeps
Stirling M. Kelso
Monica Khemsurov
Daniel Kurtz-Phelan
Whitney Lawson
Matt Lee and Ted Lee
Peter Jon Lindberg
Meg Lukens Noonan
Charles Maclean
Bruno Maddox
Jane Margolies
Francine Maroukian
Alexandra Marshall
Daniel Mendelsohn
Stephen Metcalf
Shane Mitchell
John Newton
Richard Panek
Amy Paulsen
Christopher Petkanas
Michael Pollan
Sheridan Prasso
Jeannie Ralston
Sean Rocha
Douglas Rogers
Pavia Rosati
Frank Rose
Lucinda Rosenfeld
Rory Ross
Julian Rubinstein
Alex Salkever
Bruce Schoenfeld
Helen Schulman
Oliver Schwaner-Albright
John Seabrook
Maria Shollenbarger
Alex Shoumatoff
Valerie Stivers-Isakova
Emma Sloley
Heather Smith MacIsaac
Andrew Solomon
Guy Trebay
Meeghan Truelove
Rachel Urquhart
Anya Von Bremzen
Sally Webb
Peter Weller
Sarah Wildman
Jeff Wise
Michael Z. Wise
Lynn Yaeger

Most of the stories in this book first appeared in *Travel + Leisure* magazine, and have been updated and adapted for use here. To learn more about these destinations, or to read the original stories, go to *travelandleisure.com*.

A Veramonte vineyard in Chile's Casablanca Valley.

Fishermen sailing on the Indian Ocean, just off the coast of Madagascar.

PHOTOGRAPHERS

A magazine of modern global culture, *Travel + Leisure* examines the places, ideas, and trends that define the way we travel now. T+L inspires readers to explore the world, equipping them with expert advice and a better understanding of the endless possibilities of travel. Delivering clear, comprehensive service journalism, intelligent writing, and evocative photography, T+L is the authority for today's traveler. Visit us at **travelandleisure.com.**